Praise from parenting experts...

"A helpful, hopeful approach to the parenting process. This book empowers parents by giving them the tools needed to look inside themselves for strength and guidance."
David Katzner, President, The National Parenting Center

"... unique in the simplicity of its presentation, its profound insight, and practical guidelines. This is the most critical social issue today — the nurturing of children and their parents. I sincerely hope this book is read by our whole population."
Joseph Chilton Pearce, Author, *Magical Child, Evolution's End*

"... practical, down-to-earth guide in bringing love, compassion and empathy into all human relationships, especially with children."
Larry Dossey, M.D., Author, *Healing Words*

"This is a perfect book for all parents on this planet."
Steveanne Auerbach, Ph.D., "Dr. Toy," Director,
Institute for Childhood Resources, San Francisco, CA

"... full of clear, simple responses that overcome the challenges parents face, and build a loving family experience."
***Co-operatively Speaking*, the newsletter of**
Parent Cooperative Preschools International

"Using simple, easy-to-learn, scientifically-tested techniques, Doc Lew Childre has come up with a novel approach and guide to parenting which can build self-esteem and improve communication for parents and children of all ages."
DeWitt C. Baldwin, Jr., M.D., Pediatrician, Family Physician and
Professor Emeritus of Psychology and Behavioral Sciences,
University of Nevada School of Medicine

"*A Parenting Manual* outlines a compassionate and common-sense approach to the most important and challenging endeavor a person can assume: raising another human being."
David S. Kurtz, Ph.D., Director, Childhelp USA,
National Child Abuse Hotline

Recommended by educational experts...

"*A Parenting Manual* is a remarkable, practical, down-to-earth guide that develops the whole child — mind and soul. This easy-to-understand book covers the most difficult issues of parent/child relationships. [It] is now at the top of my recommended reading list, as well as a resource for both my lectures and radio show. I recommend this book as a source of guidance for a parent who wants their child to develop a life-long love of learning with high self-esteem and self-worth. I strongly recommend that all parents of children of any age read this book."
Peter Riddle, President, Empowered Learning, Inc., host of the national radio show, *Empowered Learning with Peter Riddle*

"As president of 18-year-old Educational Book Distributors, I am unfailingly enthusiastic representing this wonderful book to the education markets. In our rapidly changing world the need to creatively relate to our children becomes paramount, and Doc Lew Childre shows us how — without 'can't' or guilt, but with heart and understanding — to help ensure our children's emotional health and growth. This book belongs in the library of every home with children."
Robert Toms, President, Educational Book Distributors

"Very practical, useful techniques . . . tools that cause me to have hope in working with some students who I have been unable to reach . . . plus energy to try."
Carol Roblauskas, District Counselor

"The HeartMath tools gave me an insight into my soul and acceptance of myself for the very first time."
Josefina Viramontes, Parent Education Specialist

"After feeling depressed and depleted of care, I have hope . . . "
Susan Scott Timmer, Elementary School Teacher

Parents talk about the results...

"I've read many . . . parenting books, but none can compare to *A Parenting Manual.* . . . Light, easy to read style . . . encompasses everything from a child's developmental stages, to where the problem is and how to solve it without guilt! A must for parents of our future generation."
Sheila Gordon, Career Consultant

"Being a single working mother of a teen boy, I learned tools that brought balance and harmony to our hectic life, and created a peaceful existence between my son and me."
Robin Jordan, Administrative Assistant

". . . tools to quickly stop destructive emotions and then discover . . . solutions to difficult situations with my family . . . simple yet effective . . ."
Rich Duke, Parent

"My family and I have experienced incredible results . . .
  1 - Loving each other more
  2 - Able to adapt to changes more effectively
  3 - Relieve stress in general
  4 - Improve personal relationships
  5 - Listening has improved
  6 - Understanding
  7 - Really appreciating what we have as individuals and as a family team
  8 - Slowing down our reactions
  9 - Appreciating our health
  10 - Communicate in a really easy manner
Kimberly Trujillo, Corporate Trainer

"I've learned that knowing my 'bottom line' and setting it are key to taking care of myself in the mothering game. And that self-care is essential to *really* being there for your kids."
Diana Govan, Parent

"Hope producing and inspiring. I no longer feel overwhelmed in my perception of what it means to be an adequate parent."
Linda Davine, Legal Secretary

BY DOC LEW CHILDRE

Self Empowerment:
The Heart Approach to Stress Management

FREEZE-FRAME:
Fast Action Stress Relief;
A Scientifically Proven Technique

FREEZE-FRAME Audiobook

CUT-THRU:
Achieve Total Security and Maximum Energy
A Scientifically Proven Insight on
How to Care Without Becoming a Victim

CUT-THRU Audiobook

The How To Book of Teen Self Discovery

A Parenting Manual:
Heart Hope for the Family

Teaching Children to Love:
55 Games and Fun Activities for
Raising Balanced Children in Unbalanced Times

Women Lead With Their Hearts:
The New Paradigm and New Solution for the 21st Century
— A White Paper —

Heart Zones (cassette and CD)

Speed of Balance (cassette and CD)

A
PARENTING
MANUAL

Heart Hope *for the* Family

by
Doc Lew Childre

Edited by Sara Hatch Paddison

PLANETARY PUBLICATIONS
Boulder Creek, California

Published in the United States of America by:

Planetary Publications
P.O. Box 66, Boulder Creek, California 95006
(800) 372-3100   (408) 338-2161   Fax (408) 338-9861

Manufactured in the United States of America by BookCrafters
First Printing 1995
Second Printing 1995

Cover Design by Sandy Royall

Library of Congress Cataloging in Publication Data
Childre, Doc Lew,   1945-
    A parenting manual : heart hope for the family / by Doc Lew Childre; edited by Sara Paddison.
        p. cm.
    Includes bibliographical references and index.
    ISBN 1-879052-32-6
    1. Child psychology. 2. Child rearing. 3. Stress in children. 4. Self-esteem in children. I. Paddison, Sara, 1953-   . II. Title.
HQ772.5.C44 1995
649' . 1--dc20
                               95-167
                               CIP

10 9 8 7 6 5 4 3 2

Table of Contents

Author's Introduction   11

Chapter 1 — What's Love Got To Do With It?   **15**

Love And Perception   17
Practicing Love   18
The ABC's of Love   18
Steps of the HEART LOCK-IN   20
Understanding Your Heart   21

Chapter 2 — Changing Our Perceptions In Today's Changing World   **25**

How Do Children Perceive Life Today?   26
What do the Statistics Say?   27
The Power of the Heart   30
A Heart Intelligence Perspective   32

Chapter 3 — Intuitive Heart Understanding   **35**

What is FREEZE-FRAME?   38
The Steps of FREEZE-FRAME   39
How Children Relate to FREEZE-FRAME   46

Chapter 4 — Managing and Improving Your Mind   **47**

Mind Processing   48
Judgments   49
Blame   52
Overcoming Judgments   54

Chapter 5 — The Impact of Stress   **57**

A Stress Epidemic   60
What's a Parent to Do?   62
A Choice   63
Head Choices   63
Heart Choices   65
Compassion   66
Transforming Repression   67

Chapter 6 — How to Care without Overcare   **69**

Check Yourself for Overcare   70
The Real Drug Problem   72
Adaptability   73
The Power of Sincere Care   75
Single Parenting   78
Hand-Me-Down Ideas   80
Women and Overcare   81
A Stand versus A Stance   82
Emotional Upsets and Heartaches   83
Practicing True Care — For Yourself and Your Child   86

Chapter 7 — Effective Communication   **89**

Communicating Discipline to Children   91
Parental Assessment   92
An Important Tool for Parenting —
    Sincere Communication and Deep Listening   94
The INTUITIVE LISTENING Tool   95
How to Apply INTUITIVE LISTENING   97
Perceptions, Actions & Consequences   98
The Importance of Structure   100
Balanced Discipline   104

Chapter 8 — The Beginning Patterns of Growth   **107**

Natural Laws and Human Growth   109
One Year Old   113
Two Years Old   113
A FREEZE-FRAME Game for Toddlers   114
Three Years Old   116
Four Years Old   117
Teaching FREEZE-FRAME to Four to Six Year Olds   119
Five and Six Years Old   120
Deep Heart Listening and Speak Your Truth   121

Chapter 9 — The Middle Years of Childhood   **123**

Discovering Individuality   124
Understanding Your Seven to Twelve Year Old's Perceptions   125
Teaching Seven to Twelve Year Olds How to FREEZE-FRAME   127
Seven Years Old   132
Eight Years Old   133
Nine Years Old   134
Ten Years Old   134
Eleven Years Old   135
Twelve Years Old   136

Chapter 10 — Understanding the Teenage Shift   **139**

Teen Statistics   140
Common Sense Solutions   143
Thirteen Years Old   145
Fourteen Years Old   146
Fifteen to Nineteen Years Old   147

Conclusion   **149**

References   **153**

Author's Introduction

Emotions out of control . . . impulsive words . . . destructive actions . . . destroyed families. The downward spiral of untreated stress is a plague touching many — perhaps most — households in the developed world. Little wonder. The life most people are living today is not the one their parents or schools prepared them for. People are scrambling for position, wondering how they'll fit in, fearful that they'll be left behind in the "human race" that is life at the turn of the 21st century.

But stress and suffering are not the inevitable result of modern life. There are always some people around who cope perfectly well as they experience the buffeting forces of change; some families that survive, even thrive, through it all. What are their coping secrets?

For years, I have researched the role of the head, the heart, and the intuition in seeking to determine the differentiating factors of human response to conditions. I developed the HeartMath® system to help people achieve continuity in mental and emotional balance and more effectively access their own intelligence. I founded the not-for-profit Institute of HeartMath (IHM), now a leading-edge research and training organization known for innovative work in the fields of human effectiveness and interaction. IHM tools, such as FREEZE-

FRAME®, are being used successfully by Fortune 500 corporate clients, as well as by government departments, all four branches of the US military, and in the places where their effectiveness was first proven: in prisons and among Los Angeles gang youth.

How does it work? Well, it's like this: when a person will just *stop* for one minute and apply HeartMath techniques — and one minute is all it takes — they have a greater likelihood of hearing their intuition. Intuition is smart, and it's fast. Given less than a minute, this high speed, innate intelligence we call intuition (or common sense) will advise you on the appropriate course of action. The trouble is that today, even one minute can sometimes seem like a long time. That is why books like this one are needed: just to remind you to take that minute, that FREEZE-FRAME minute. And to advise you in some detail on exactly what to do with that minute to save yourself and your family.

Adults and children are using this one-minute technique to reduce stress, reduce emotional pain, develop more sensitive communications, improve their relationships, save time, save energy, and generally make life a much more enjoyable experience. Try it. You'll find you're happier. You'll stop *reacting* and start the habit of quickly accessing a sudden shift in your perception of things, a shift that will invariably bring appropriate new solutions into focus. No more bitter complaints about co-workers, no more blowing up at your kids, parents, or spouse. With practice, you simply won't do those things anymore.

Many parents who have read one of my books, *The How To Book of Teen Self Discovery, Self-Empowerment,* or *FREEZE-FRAME,* have asked me how to teach HeartMath to children. From a young age, I realized that happiness and self-empowerment result more from inner attitude than from educational degrees, jobs, or financial success. I have helped raise six children and counseled people of all ages. I've met many frustrated and confused children who see no hope for the future. They simply don't know which direction to take. Most are searching for love, but feel they have to find it on their own. Children perceive that, "adults don't have it together" and therefore can't demonstrate to them how to love. I wrote *A Parenting Manual* to convey both my understanding of child development and to instruct parents how to use HeartMath tools with children so they can "keep it together" in a rapidly shifting world. HeartMath shows people how to perceive through the heart. It is the heart that brings love, hope, and a more fulfilling life. Parenting is a difficult job in these changing times. It's important not to look for perfection as you practice HeartMath, but to look for increasing ratios of actualization and fulfillment versus stress and ineffectiveness.

Those of you who have read my other books will recognize some of the research cited here. These discoveries are central to my thesis on parenting, as they were to our IHM work on the teen years and on the FREEZE-FRAME practice in general. Each chapter of this book offers step-by-step instruction in the use of HeartMath tools from the particular perspective of the parent-child and child-parent relationships. You will learn how to achieve mental and emotional balance, how to understand children's feelings and how to provide effective discipline. Please know that the guidance offered can be applied by anyone; mother, father, grandparent, step-parent, un-related guardian, or other adult. I mention scientific research conducted at IHM and other institutions in a user-friendly way. I've referenced only those studies that are most relevant. If you want to order our scientific papers or receive more information, please contact IHM.

A Parenting Manual provides a stark picture of the stress overload and struggles many adults and children experience in today's society. Throughout the book, I refer to numerous examples, statistics, surveys, and polls of parents, teenagers, and children. In some examples, the names have been changed to protect people's privacy. While any one statistic may not appear significant, taken together they point to an extremely serious crisis of disaffected young people — a crisis that will not go away without practical new tools for both children and adults.

Emotional challenges truly won't harm children if they are taught how to handle them. Children need experiences where they can succeed and gain a sense of their own worth. It's a parent's responsibility to help the child be happy and succeed. Many parents honestly don't know how to do this. Children of the '90s perceive life quite differently from how we adults perceived life when we were children. *Effective parenting starts with first seeing how your child perceives.* Ponder this as you read. Consider how each HeartMath tool might apply to your own situation, then try it out. Have fun discovering your own heart intelligence. Through sincere practice, you will see how productive it can be to apply HeartMath tools to yourself and teach them to your child — increasing the quality of both your lives.

Doc Lew Childre
Boulder Creek, California

Chapter 1

What's Love Got To Do With It?

What is love and from where does it come? People have asked that question for thousands of years. Love and the heart have always been closely related, but only now is science beginning to explain why. People hold feelings of love close to their hearts. Love imparts the loyalty and responsibility a parent feels for a child. Love also brings understanding. A parent who loves a child becomes intuitively aware of that child's needs. Sincere loving by the parent automatically establishes an *intuitional field of knowingness* between the parent and the child.

In the area of love, the child may sometimes lead the parent, but only when the basic love relationship is already in place. The child is your apprentice in this guild of love. As the parent, your job is to teach intuitive understanding as if it were a science and a skill (actually, it is). This book is about how to do that.

A child develops healthy perceptions and excels if the parent practices being a conscious and consistent model of love. Love is the configuration for effectively communicating with a child of any age. Babies are exceptionally sensitive. They may not comprehend the words, but they hear and feel the love. By acquiring the knowledge to *consciously* love, parents access a superior intuitional frequency within their own innate intelligence. This quickens the intuitive connection with their baby, toddler, teen, or grown-up child.

Loving parents, by their very nature, provide children with a secure atmosphere in which to perceive life as a series of challenges that build confidence, rather than as a progression of unsolvable problems that destroy self-worth. Most parents love their children, but feel that love isn't enough to raise a child these days. A neighbor, Ann, used to visit me and say how much she loved her little Joey, but then would gripe about endless flare-ups and judge him. I thought, "Ann, stop complaining and nagging Joey. Try loving him more." A child needs a heart-intelligent parent more than a head-knowing parent. Ann didn't know *how* to love Joey effectively. Ann isn't alone. Many mothers and fathers feel Ann's inner tug-of-war, dismayed that their love isn't solving their child's problems.

If our days are stressful and our minds occupied, love hardly has a chance. We assume we are functioning from a loving place, yet persist in subtly or overtly judging our children, our spouses, or ourselves. To love effectively, we must consciously practice addressing life with love. Love can turn around difficult situations that might otherwise blow up. We've all experienced occasions of that. An IHM staff member told me a story that left an impression on her since age three: *"My parents were outside in the backyard arguing about my older brother. I was fussing, whining, pestering my parents. After a considerable amount of interruptions, my father said, 'Now just stop it! That's enough! Straighten up and get on the ball!' I stood straight as an arrow and looked around in bewilderment. 'Where is the ball, Daddy?' I asked. To my surprise, I received a round of warm laughter and a big hug."*

Experiencing and expressing love are the peak moments of fulfillment in life. How wonderful that love can be experienced through so many feelings and qualities! A child's love for her mom or dad has a safe, secure, calming feeling. Her love for her sister has a different quality. Sisters may argue and fight, but the sisterly feeling is a bond that underlies the ups and downs and is sustained through the years. Sibling bonding feels different from the love felt for a friend. A good friend's love is there when you need it, but often circumstances and interests take you and your friends in different directions. Love for the Earth offers yet another feeling, a connection with nature, animals, flowers, trees, the sky, the soil. Feelings of love can be expansive, explosive, or energizing. Love is also caring, forgiving, appreciative, and compassionate. The bottom line is this — love embraces, fulfills, and rewards. Without love, prosperity seems incomplete. Most educators and our own common sense agree that a loving environment is the most beneficial for learning. In my experience, it's love that unfolds the gift of self-empowerment.

Love and Perception

You can address life as a process of realization about your child by utilizing your heart intelligence. By consciously practicing love, a parent can intuitionally protect and guide the child into the proper angles of perception. Quality heart time is provided to encourage the child, without the head energies that cause excessive overprotection, constant stimulation, or nullify your bottom-line boundaries. Be creative; encourage enterprising growth. Respectfully and with love, lead your child into unfamiliar situations.

A physical and spiritual drive toward growth dwells within all children. Growth challenges a child to depart from the known and travel into the unknown. This implies uncertainty, so movement into the unknown can trigger anxiety. Love allows perceptions of life to unfold in an atmosphere of hope and security. A child, ages zero to seven, who learns to inhabit the Earth in a field of love will not experience the internal suffering we call *frustration* when moving through difficult passages in life. It's parental love and care that make mastering the early knowledge of motor skills a fun event instead of a

17

growing pain. Providing safe experiences translates as love-in-action for any child. Love prompts parents to re-examine the home climate they provide. Setting boundaries with the heart intuition is solid care that enhances a child's growth pattern. As security is established, a child will self-validate and self-empower.

Practicing Love

For as long as humanity can remember, people have conversed about love, sung about love, written about love. Romance novels have remained the #1 best sellers for decades, overflowing shelves in airports, supermarkets, and bookstores. Throughout the centuries, the world's cultures have philosophized about love and its power. From the old testament to the bibles of all major religions, love is glorified. What would occur if love were sincerely, consistently, and actively practiced?

While love is often applauded, there is a line of distinction between *imagining love* and *honestly practicing* love. People usually love only as the mood arises or if their day is going especially well. Love is most often kindled by children at poignant moments, by friends on occasion, or with a romantic partner. By consciously loving, you harmonize the foundational heart energy in yourself and in your family. Sensitivity increases, communication grows clearer, and understanding develops. Love changes the atmospheric condition of a child's environment. When love is sincerely, consistently, and actively practiced, it spawns hope — *heart hope for the family.*

The ABC's of Love

We are correctly taught in school that practice precedes effectiveness, whether in reading, writing, computers, or any skill. But we are rarely taught *how* to practice love. Therefore, most people tap only a small percentage of the power of love. Here are the ABC's of how to love:

The first step in practicing love is to know that the heart is a source of strength and power. The heart's power is different from the head's. You use your head to memorize, analyze, read words, and think. You use your heart to feel feelings like care, appreciation, joy, and love. Without a heart to feel love, life isn't fun. Apply love with the intent of a trail blazer navigating new territory. A technique to do this is called the "HEART LOCK-IN" (instructions are on the next page.) This is a powerful means of connecting with your heart that you can use at any time to construct a deeper understanding of love.

Parents who practice HEART LOCK-INs report many benefits. They find it helps release tension and anxiety and smoothes out many rough edges in relating to their children. One parent proclaimed, *"I was so surprised that practicing love in this way helped me find a flow through the ups and downs of juggling work, family, and the constant demands on my time. I really feel less stressed and the major problems I was having with my five year old son have resolved. I'm simply calmer and can see what to do, instead of worrying about whether I'm doing the right thing all the time."*

HEART LOCK-INs are easy to add to a busy schedule. An elementary school teacher reported effective, time-saving results: *"Practicing a HEART LOCK-IN and sending five minutes of love to a difficult child for five days in a row greatly changed that child's behavior and it also changed my reactions to the child. Previously that child had been taking up a large portion of my time."*

Steps of the HEART LOCK-IN:

1. Find a comfortable place to relax for five to fifteen minutes and close your eyes.

2. Shift your attention away from your mind or head, relax your thoughts, and focus in the area around your heart, that place where you have felt deep feelings of sincere love, care, or appreciation.

3. Remember a special experience you've had with your child, when the feeling of love, care, or appreciation was rewarding. Recall the feeling. If you're upset with your child, it may be harder to recall a special feeling. Try to remember when you felt a joy of delight, perhaps when your baby was in your arms or when the "little angel" was asleep.

4. Radiate that sincere feeling of love to your child now; this energizes the love fully and gives you a more complete understanding of your child.

5. If head thoughts come in, gently bring your focus of attention back to the heart area and radiate love from the heart. Just by sending heart, your questions will eventually be answered. Loving your child builds patience and brings understanding.

6. Now, radiate love to your child for five to fifteen minutes to deepen the LOCK-IN. Reflect on what you love about your child, then radiate that feeling of love. It does not require words. This "locks" you into a feeling of love in the heart, appreciation for your child, and gives access to intuitive information. As you listen to your heart intuition, it helps sustain feelings of love and fulfillment. The rewards of parenting come quickly with a little sincere effort.

If you are having a difficult time with your child and you can't immediately remember and recall a feeling of love, care, or appreciation, or if you feel some pain in your heart, it's okay. With practice, the HEART LOCK-IN will increase positive feelings and release insecure, painful feelings stored in the unconscious to bring you to a solid heart security. Security is what finally transforms pain and old hurts. As love expands in quality, the old attitudes and feelings release in stages. View all feelings that arise during a HEART LOCK-IN as love that is growing but that is perhaps not yet complete in its full quality.

While busy with daily activities, try to recall the positive feelings you experienced while locking into the heart. Do mini HEART LOCK-INs for a few minutes, once or twice during the work day, to energize the feelings of love. As intuitive thoughts come to you that are accompanied by a sense of inner knowingness or peace, write them down to remember to act on them. This will help you practice following your heart intuition with more continuity. Test the wisdom of what you perceive from the heart to see if it brings you more peace and understanding. Notice if it helps your relationship with your child.

Understanding Your Heart

Webster's Dictionary defines the "heart" as: 1. A hollow, muscular organ which by rhythmic contraction and relaxation keeps the blood in circulation throughout the body. 2. The center of the total personality, especially with reference to intuition, feeling, or emotion. 3. The center of emotion, especially as contrasted to the head as the seat of intellect. 4. Spirit, courage, enthusiasm. 5. The innermost or central part of anything. 6. The vital or essential part, the core.[1]

I once watched a toddler play with some colorful balls. He was fascinated by them, giggling with delight as he pranced around, bouncing the balls high into the air. I saw that toddler putting his full spirit and enthusiasm — *his heart* — into his play. This is not the version of "heart" most adults know. Most see the heart as sad, fragile, mushy, emotional, a heart that can break, be victimized. However, the qualities and feelings of the True Heart are: a source of strength, clarity, knowing, power, care, compassion, wisdom, love, courage, peace, and joy. The intelligence of the heart is where clarity and vitality feed us fulfillment. These values held in the heart expand as wisdom.

But wait a minute. Aren't all these references to heart just figures of speech? When we talk about the heart in these ways, there's no relationship to the "hollow, muscular organ," is there?

Yes, there is. It is more than a coincidence that people have spoken of "the heart" in these ways for centuries. Research we have done at the Institute of HeartMath has proven that the physical heart, that "hollow, muscular organ" — is indeed a seat of many of the most important human qualities.

IHM has been engaged in several areas of scientific investigation that correlate a person's mental, emotional, and behavioral states with the heart's electrical system, the autonomic nervous system, and the immune and hormonal systems. The results of this research are validating what common sense, intuitive intelligence tells us: that our perceptions, mental and emotional attitudes, our immune system, our reaction times, and our decision-making abilities, are all directly related to the health of our heart.

Forgiveness, appreciation, and love are caring qualities in action. IHM research is showing that these positive attitudes and qualities actually lead to coherent, harmonious heart rhythms and affect the physical heart's electrical output, as seen in the analysis of the electrocardiogram (ECG).[2] These sincere positive feelings generate coherent heart frequencies which are felt by every cell in the body. Other research has shown that positive feelings boost the immune system.[3] Therefore, it's important to ask ourselves, *"How can we increase the quantity of these positive feelings and qualities? How do we help children increase their positive feelings and best qualities?"*

In the past decade, scientists have discovered that repeated stressful reactions, such as frustration and anger, cause nervous system imbalances which are detrimental not only to the physical heart, but to the brain, hormonal, and immune systems. Even remembering an upsetting experience can reduce the heart's pumping efficiency by 5-7%.[4] Other research at IHM has shown that remembering upsetting experiences also depletes the immune system for many hours. IHM researchers found that just one, five-minute episode of mentally and emotionally recalling an experience of anger and frustration caused a depletion in Immunoglobulin A (IgA) for the next six hours.[5] IgA is an immune system antibody and one of the body's first lines of defense against colds, flu, and infections. How many parents, how many people, deplete their immune systems daily with real-time anger and frustration, not to mention rehashing stressful thoughts and feelings throughout a day? A daily diet of these upsetting experiences drains us and strains our relationship with our children.

Figure (1) Stress-Producing | Figure (2) Stress-Reducing

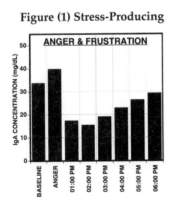
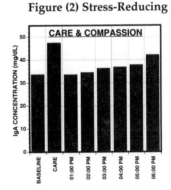

Figure (1) and (2) illustrate the effect that feeling care and compassion (right) had on the experimental group's average IgA levels throughout the day. There was an immediate and significant increase in IgA, and while it dropped back to normal an hour later, IgA levels continued to increase throughout the rest of the day. Individuals experiencing a 5-minute period of anger and frustration (left) had an immediate increase in IgA. However, a dramatic decrease in IgA levels followed, and lasted throughout the day, showing the powerful effects even one episode of recalling an experience of anger can have on the immune system. This may explain why some people say they "feel better" after blowing their top. But they pay a day-long price later on.

On the other hand, the same IgA study showed that one, five-minute episode of genuinely feeling care or compassion enhances the immune system. Five minutes of sincerely feeling care or compassion for someone caused a gradual climb in IgA over the next six hours. This love and care is the most advantageous medicine known.

Other scientific studies have shown that feelings of happiness and joy benefit white blood cells needed for healing and defense against invading pathogens, including cancer and virus-infected cells.[6] Thus a major contributing factor to poor health and rising health care costs may be the lack of love, care, happiness, and joy in our society.

There are moments in most people's lives when they feel their hearts come alive, and they feel happy and fulfilled. Their lives have meaning in these peak experiences. Children have many of these experiences, but the number seems to dwindle as they lose their child-like spirit. A four year old can gaze in awestruck wonder at a glorious sunset, a field of flowers, or the nighttime sky. As we grow older and become enmeshed in the stressors of everyday life, we may not even notice the night sky. Or it becomes dull to our overall perception. As you learn to live in the heart and *consciously* love, you create beneficial changes in your hormonal balance and health, beneficial changes in your perceptions and interactions with others, and you can live in love with life. The HeartMath principles show adults and children, even at an early age, how to use the common sense of the heart to understand the consequences and challenges of life. The heart brings good feelings and astonishing intelligence.

Chapter 2

Changing Our Perceptions In Today's Changing World

The world is in an unprecedented state of flux. Borders are changing. Beliefs are changing. Political systems are changing. Families are changing. No one knows for sure what the future will bring. Many say a "global paradigm shift" is occurring. A paradigm shift is a fundamental change in the way masses of people *perceive* life. There are many examples of paradigm shifts throughout history. People once thought the sun rotated around the Earth. When Galileo proved the opposite, a new era of science was born out of this radically new perception. The Industrial Age was a paradigm shift from an agrarian lifestyle to a mechanistic lifestyle. The invention of the light bulb, telephones, the automobile, airplanes, all dramatically altered the way people related to and perceived each other. The atomic age, ushering in television, microsurgery, electronics, and threat of nuclear war, further modernized human perception, for better or for worse.

For masses of people in the '90s, the bombardment of information from all over the globe is forcing rapid adjustments in how we perceive, live, and relate to each other. Life is moving faster for adults and children alike. Imagine the constant input children get from the new information highways — TV, movies, video games, computers,

CD-ROMS, satellite communication systems, etc.

The media constantly discharge unfiltered information to our children. Much of this information overstimulates children, causing insecurity, fear, and stress. Countless TV programs and movies, from cop shows to cartoons to action "thrillers," depict violence as the preferred solution when conflicts arise. There are sixteen acts of violence per hour on children's programming, only eight per hour on adults'. By the time they are teens, children have seen an estimated 18,000 violent murders on TV.[7] Rapid fire information without enough knowledge on how to assimilate it creates overload — which equals stressed and unhappy children and adults. The ability of children to find balanced perspectives about life is being stretched to the limit. A little compassion is in order for today's generation. With compassion comes hope — hope that brings new heart-intelligent solutions.

How Do Children Perceive Life Today?

I did a survey of dozens of children from different cultural backgrounds, ages six to seventeen. I asked the following questions: Who are you? Where are you going? How do you see life? How do you think other kids see life? How do you think adults see life? Here are a few responses.

"I'm Brittany. I'm seven. I like life. I like Lake Tahoe and the snow. I like my uncle's and aunt's new baby. I feel sad because my friend moved away. Some people are sad, some are happy. Some people make others sad."

"I'm Elliot, age ten. I like my life. It's cool and I love my mom a lot and the same thing with my dad and my sister, too, and my baby brother. I hate violence that is going around the city."

"I'm Angie. I'm sixteen. I like life. Of course there are those days that aren't good and then there is school. It's trying and tiring at times. I can't wait 'til the weekends because there is no school and you can go out and do things like see friends, stay out later on weekends.

Some kids think life sucks, others think it's great. There are all sorts of pressures these days from school, parents, sex, drugs. I think adults are very stressed out. I think a lot love their kids, but many of them aren't very caring towards them."

The younger children I surveyed, ages six to eight, perceived life as fun, but only if everything was all right in the family. If it was not, then they often said life was sad and lonely. Children ages nine to twelve perceived life as unpredictable. They worried about violence and feeling safe. Angie's answers were typical of many teens. While some children thirteen to seventeen were excited about life and about their future, the majority perceived life pessimistically. I conducted this survey because I wanted to know what children are really feeling. In spite of the fact that the economy is growing, employment is at an all-time high, and America is still one of the freest societies in the world, for many, the quality of life is getting worse. Their prevailing perception is that life is bleak and there is no solution. A clear picture has emerged of a society where adults and children are confused, and heart management of our perceptions is dramatically lacking.

What Do The Statistics Say?

Surveys conducted in 1994 reveal that many children in the U.S. live across a deep divide from their parents. Reading these statistics could strengthen or weaken our resolve to find practical solutions, depending on how we perceive them. This book offers hopeful alternatives, ones that can begin to change our perceptions of our children, our society, and ourselves.

- According to the Children's Defense Fund: Almost 20% of children in the U.S., ages six to twelve, haven't had even a ten minute conversation with a parent in a month.

- Seven million children are "latchkey kids," where no one is home when they return from school each day.

- Only 3% of teens prefer the company of someone in their family; 40% say their parents are often unavailable to them — whether their mothers work outside the home or not.

- Nearly 60% of youngsters surveyed nationwide said they worried about becoming a victim of violence at school.

- Over 80% of teens are worried about violence, drinking, guns, sex, drugs, and getting a good job.

- Very few teens express moral qualms about drinking or cheating; 35% regularly drink alcohol; 80% expect the problems to get worse; and 60% have contemplated suicide.

Where is this hopelessness springing from? What perceptions cause many teens to behave like wounded humans instead of like loving people? Children reflect what they see modeled by their parents, teachers and other adult figures. We clearly have to shed our tired old perceptions if we want our kids to grow into responsible, mature and caring adults.

The fear of violence that children feel is often real; it is our responsibility as adults to offer tools that create environments based on love, understanding, and true community. With heart perception, we gain balanced perspectives about how to deal with these tough issues. The issues will not magically disappear, but our creativity and resiliency in dealing with them will increase exponentially as we discover the power of heart intelligence.

When both parents work, children coming home to an empty house is often unavoidable. Yet if the environment they return to is one of love and respect, children's security can grow. Our society is filled with stories of people who have created successful, fulfilled lives out of poor or disadvantaged upbringings. How we perceive "the hand we've been dealt" is the key to our success or failure.

These statistics and many others simply reflect symptoms of a disease, a societal disease of limited perception. Many children see no way out of their hopeless perspectives. We have unknowingly taught our children to perceive life through fearful, angry, insecure eyes. Their hopelessness reflects the perceptions of society around them. As one young man told me, *"Why shouldn't kids feel a lot of pain? There's nothing to do. Everything's falling apart. It's every person for himself."* A myriad of occurrences have increased fear, stress, and turmoil in children — drug dealing, drive-by shootings, more people than ever on welfare, more people homeless, sexual exploitation, an epidemic of teen pregnancies, and constant reports of rapes, murders, and abuse. The cure for these problems is a paradigm shift to heart perception, leading to loving, caring and effective action.

Just as we can look at life from the perspective of pain, misery and hopelessness, we can also choose perspectives that encourage creative growth, hopefulness, and love. Children are incredibly receptive to positive perspectives when offered with sincerity and common sense. It is only when hopeful perspectives are absent that children grow into hardened, cynical adults, and so the cycle continues. As adults in this world, it is our responsibility to offer knowledge and know-how on how to respond to stressful situations. Parents choose this responsibility by having a baby. But parents need society's help and support.

The other day, I was standing in line at a grocery store watching a five year old testing his mother. He wanted some bubble gum and she wouldn't let him have it. He raised a ruckus and she kept hissing "shut-up." The adults standing by shook their heads at the mother with judgmental stares that said, "It's all your fault." The mother left her groceries, grabbed her kid and rushed out of the store. I thought to myself, if only more adults knew how to love *actively*, this world would be a far better place. It doesn't help when we point the finger in blame at parents or teachers, saying it's their problem. The rising statistics on youth violence, substance abuse, gangs, and illiteracy are all saying that it's *our* problem. My intent in writing this book is to provide hopeful new solutions that address the inescapable fact that *all negativity is a result of perception and our inability to manage ourselves mentally and emotionally so we <u>can</u> see another reality.*

The Power of the Heart

In my years of research on stress and behavior, I realized that the missing segment in stress reduction, values education, or self-help programs is a knowledge of the power of the heart. The heart is actually designed to play the starring role in overall consciousness. The main thing to master while growing up is how to use the power of one's own heart as an unlimited source of commonsense wisdom and intuition for making efficient choices in life. Teaching children to understand their own internal feedback signals — with heart intelligence — can solve the challenges of our times.

Adults speak sentimentally of children as, "The hope for the future." However, children of the '90s are the first generation in America to scream, "We feel no hope!" New tools are clearly needed. Children need tools to perceive that: *Stress is an untransformed opportunity for self-empowerment and self-security — a challenge rather than a threat.*

In the '60s, many teens felt a sense of hope and purpose. Even in a decade that saw the assassination of many leaders — President Kennedy, Martin Luther King, Bobby Kennedy, and Malcolm X — the spirit of hope was still high. The hippie attire and lifestyle of free love were a rebellion against parental values, but also a statement of idealism that the youth were going to change the world. Each decade seems to make its own statement. Most offspring of hippies and "baby boomers" were teens in the late '70s and '80s. The extreme statement then was punk and grunge. Now twenty to thirty years old, they are called "baby busters" or "generation X." Often pessimistic and cynical, they feel their future has been mortgaged by social security, a huge national debt, and a lack of good jobs. Perception, once again, is at the root of the malaise.

In the mid '90s, the standard mode of dress for kids eleven to nineteen is a baseball cap worn backwards with baggy shirts and jeans. Can we decipher what statement these teens are making? Is it a request for a more casual lifestyle? Are they saying, "Life is a joke, because we don't know how else to think about it?" Or, are teens really saying, "We don't know which direction to go, or what to do, or how to care? Life seems pointless so far." What values are going to change the downward spiral of cynicism that is being passed on to our youth? Too much stress creates hopelessness and pessimism. As I see it, children need help to deal with personal and societal stress, to *rise above it all and see from a more hopeful perspective.* They need new tools to understand and activate the core values of the heart to find renewed strength, clarity, love, courage, and compassion. They can't wait for society to change for the better. They need tools now.

As a parent today, you too need effective tools to release stress and broaden perception during the paradigm shift. If anger surges inside you and you scream or slap your child, she is learning that is how you deal with frustration or stress. Fifteen year old Dana told me the following account, *"One of my friends, a senior who's smart and sweet, got into an argument with her mom in front of me and two other friends. Her mom screamed and started to raise her hand and so my friend slapped her out of fear. Her mom then grabbed the back of her hair and beat her, then my friend kneed her and left. It really shocked me."*

Frustrated parents need to make peace with the choice and commitment they made to have a child. Some feel trapped, as if they were serving a twenty-year prison sentence. It doesn't have to be that way. It is possible to retain your individuality and find inner peace and fulfillment as you learn new ways to love and raise your child during this global paradigm shift.

Scenes like Dana witnessed are not uncommon. Stressful reactions stimulate hormones to prepare you for "fight or flight," which means either to react aggressively or to flee from a situation. This is a necessary defense mechanism if you are in real danger; however, it does not resolve the type of stress many people feel today. Nor does it prevent or remedy communication gaps between people. Whether a person battles with someone or withdraws, depends on the person's perspective and personality trait. If you were in a child's or teenager's shoes today, what would you do? Thousands of children are joining gangs, taking drugs, or drinking alcohol to escape their stress. Many don't see any better options.

Each person must learn they have a choice to buy into a picture of gloom or gain a realistic mature understanding of why children and adults perceive the way they do. With all the fast-paced changes occurring, it's no wonder many parents simply don't know how to parent anymore. When perceptions are dragged down by society's and the media's constant trumpeting of the negative, then hopeful opportunities in life are missed. With heart management and tools to quickly broaden perception, we can do better. With heart perception, the world looks far less bleak than the statistics convey. A world of wonder, unimagined potential, and adventure is surrounding our children; through the heart they can find it.

A Heart Intelligence Perspective

Common sense says it will take a power stronger than people's habitual thoughts and perceptions in order to transform their stresses. In the heart resides the place of contact for this source of power. *Heart power is the electricity of one's inner strength and potential.* This is the power that establishes the self-motivating ability to manifest and complete oneself in achieving balance and fulfillment. This is the power required to change the stress-producing perspectives and attitudes of this world.

As you learn to view life from your heart perceptions, an intelligence hidden within your own heart will unfold. What is heart intelligence? Child development specialist and author of the book, *Evolution's End,* Joseph Chilton Pearce offers his perspective, "The affairs of the heart are directly connected to the brain and it's the heart's natural intelligence that must be unfolded for the brain to operate with greater efficiency."[7]

The heart is indeed an extremely intelligent system. The source of the heartbeat is within the heart itself and the heart maintains its own innate sense of rhythm. The physical heart has an electrical field forty to sixty times more powerful than the electrical field of the brain. Electrical signals are sent from the heart to the brain which actually alter and expand brain function.[8]

The natural intelligence of the heart is often called intuition, the "still small voice," an inner knowingness, wisdom, or just plain common sense. Intuition means to "see into it," a knowledge or understanding that comes from inside yourself. The heart contains an intelligence different from the mind — one that is designed to look after, or take care of, our entire unconscious and conscious system. Heart intelligence embraces head intelligence and is the prime, bottom-line strength of your existence. It is a class of intelligence that feels like tangible intuition — clear and efficient.

The global paradigm shift to a more humane, cooperative and loving world will be facilitated as people first make a paradigm shift within — from head to heart intelligence. The growing negativity arising from our inefficient perceptions about society, our children, and ourselves has shaken many of us loose from our traditional ways of thinking. More than ever before, people are examining the very assumptions that have propelled their lives, both personally and professionally. This self-reflection of ordinary people recognizing that there are more efficient ways to perceive and respond to life, will herald the most powerful paradigm shift of all — the shift to the domain of heart perception. This will not be led by corporations implementing bold new technology or by the changing demographic conditions in our culture. It will begin in the individual and in the family. *Heart intelligence is the hope for the 21st century.*

Remember that the intelligence of the heart must be developed. If the intellect alone is developed and children fail to expand the heart's intelligence, they become susceptible to a novelty-seeking stressful mind that functions without regard to their own or others' well-being.[7]

Heart intelligence renews hope. It represents the essence of the inner child and the responsible adult in a balanced package. Is this not the package we would like to give our children?

HeartMath is an organized arrangement of intuitive intelligence that people already have inside, but most haven't been able to access or act on that information with continuity. HeartMath provides psychological equations based on common sense — the math and science of living from the heart. It facilitates both child and parent in seeing they really do have a choice in how they perceive life.

The HeartMath system has had a wonderful impact on the lives of many adults, children, and families. It has been validated in schools, with at-risk youth, and in homes. The examples are potent. Here are just two: An eleven year old who had been on an antidepressant drug told his doctor he now had HeartMath tools that worked to release his stress, so he didn't need the drug anymore. The doctor saw the change and agreed. An extremely disruptive five year old would beat up other kids and scream relentlessly. His parents said he had never gone more than twelve hours without a screaming fit. His teacher taught him how to FREEZE-FRAME and for the next month she was astounded by his vastly improved behavior. Children are more flexible than adults so they often have quick results. Many are *starving for tools to help themselves and find new hope.*

There are many books and programs on "empowerment" offered today. Some define empowerment as giving official or legal power or authority to another, enabling or endowing them with an ability. In our research, true empowerment comes from within. *Empowerment is receiving the power to amplify consciousness and clear perception of our world.* Self-empowerment is a process that starts with understanding. It involves recognizing the inner power of the heart available to you and discovering how to direct your energy in ways beneficial to yourself and others. A fundamental shift in perspectives and attitudes will occur as adults and children open their minds to new heart perceptions. Children will follow our lead.

Chapter 3

Intuitive Heart Understanding

Intuition is one of the most sought after, highly regarded, yet elusive faculties for parents or anyone. Intuition is the emergence of clear feeling and perception, establishing a sense of heart knowingness. People assume that intuition is a flash of insight from the mind. What research is indicating is that heart frequencies transmit illumination to the higher perceptual centers in the brain, then the feelings twinkle with the "Ah-ha!" The mind then creates the thoughts or images that give meaning to the intuition and spawn understanding. The heart is an appropriate access point for bringing forth the supreme qualities of the spirit.

"Intuitive heart understanding" is a person's common-sense guidance through life. Our research has proven that a more hopeful perspective is indeed possible — one that realistically considers the serious facts but also has an intuitive heart understanding that provides more options. To achieve intuitive understanding with children, adults need to first observe — to perceive how children are perceiving. Only when you know how your own and other children are truly seeing can you begin to help them understand another point of view. This intuitive understanding can greatly ease the struggle of raising children.

There is a silent implied order in which communication occurs without words. The energy that is conveyed is really a state of consciousness. A baby can intuitively sense the inner virtue of a person. Watch a baby seemingly stare into the eyes of a new person to experience their energies. You can be talking or cooing to a baby and she'll just keep staring at you, wide-eyed, until she's satisfied; then she'll respond with a smile or cry or look away.

A mother communicates with her baby by means of the intuitive heart. This can be enacted by love, sometimes an expression without words and sentences. When a baby is three months old, the words a mother utters are sound packages that the baby feels. Talk loving mumbo-jumbo for thirty minutes and a baby will listen with focused attention and appreciate the nourishment. When a two year old first begins to talk in phrases, he'll say "gimme" or "mama, I wan yo." Through love and care, the mother hears the child's meaning and fills in the missing words. "I know, you want some yogurt," mama replies, affirming that she understands. The toddler smiles and nods. Communicating with a child is a continuous progression in parenthood. The more that parents respect children, the further they will perceive intuitionally how their child sees.

The over-examining and talking of ideas to yourself or someone else, causes words to predominate over feelings. For example, when a husband and wife become habituated in word communication about the kids, work, household issues, or each other, the underlying feelings are often overridden. Add the internal thoughts and mind chatter, and you can comprehend why people can scarcely feel the intuitional frequencies. Most people are worn out from the static of constant mental rendering which wipes out feeling the intuitive signals. The result is continual uncertainty.

Human intelligence potentially spans a wide spectrum of frequencies. The mind represents only a portion of available human intelligence. Intuition is from an additional octave of intelligence which is introduced to the mind through heart frequencies of love, compassion, appreciation, etc. This intuitive heart intelligence provides and amplifies creativity, quick problem-solving, and accurate choices. Research is showing that when individuals use the HeartMath tool FREEZE-FRAME and report intuitive "ah-ha's," heart and brain frequencies synchronize and frequency-lock.[9]

Many children are intuitively sensitive to people close to them. A child who is in her heart can know when a parent or buddy needs a kind word, a hug, or some friendly conversation. When she can help in this way, it builds confidence in her heart knowingness and confirms her intuition. Children can also use intuition to assist them in resisting peer pressure. Thirteen year old Scott uses his intuition to know where to draw the line and say no. He told me, *"The times I usually get in trouble are when I don't listen to myself. I just kind of know inside."*

Even on the physical level, the heart is an unusual organ. Heart cells play a unique dual role. They contract and expand rhythmically to pump blood and they communicate with their fellow cells. Researchers have found if two heart cells are placed near each other, they soon synchronize and beat in unison. They don't have to touch, they can communicate across a spatial barrier.[7] [10] The heart, which is composed of billions of such extraordinary cells operating in unison, is under the guidance of a higher, non-local intelligence. Those heart cells communicate through a mutually, non-localized interactive relationship via a more universal field of intelligence, which is a larger, non-physical heart — creative consciousness itself. Perhaps this explains why so many religions point to the heart as the seat of the soul.

Intui-Technology® research and training is a division of IHM dedicated to understanding heart power from all angles, then translating that comprehension into a system of self-empowerment. Intuition develops to the degree that conscious effort is made to develop and actualize it. A child practicing FREEZE-FRAME learns to discriminate heart intelligence from emotional impulses, and to generate and receive intuitive thoughts to make better choices. The process is similar to developing any skill, like learning to play a musical instrument. It requires some basic instruction and practice. Understand that it takes time to change a child's perspective. The key is to stay a step ahead in understanding your children; then you have the ability to guide them through the challenges and bumps in life. As you practice the tools offered in this book, results will come in stages. Success is increasing your ratio of fulfillment versus stress.

FREEZE-FRAME is a technique that can be used by both parent and child to acquire heart intelligence. Through Freeze-Framing, children learn how to observe, shift perspectives, and unearth thoughts that help them understand their feelings. This gives children the comfort and the comprehension that they really do have a choice.

What is FREEZE-FRAME?

A child is acquiring knowledge to become the director of his or her own life. Freeze-Framing can help anyone direct their own life more intelligently. To FREEZE-FRAME, stop your movie of life for a moment. Go to the heart for direction. It's similar to pushing the pause button on a VCR. It is actually stopping life's movie to recreate an improved reality in the moment. Stop the movie — still-frame — and ask your heart for direction. The next perception chosen will activate the next scene in the movie. People are creating their own movie by their perception and choice in each moment.

Here are the steps and instructions of FREEZE-FRAME. Mark the page so you can refer to it as you need it.

The Steps of FREEZE-FRAME

1. Recognize a stressful feeling, and FREEZE-FRAME it. Take a time out!

2. Make a sincere effort to shift your focus away from the racing mind or disturbed emotions to the area around your heart. Pretend you're breathing through your heart to help focus your energy in this area. Keep your focus there for ten seconds or more.

3. Recall a positive fun feeling or time you've had in life and attempt to re-experience it.

4. Now, using your intuition, common sense, and sincerity — ask your heart — what would be a more efficient response to the situation, one that will minimize future stress?

5. Listen to what your heart says in answer to your question. (It's an effective way to put your reactive mind and emotions in check — and an "in-house" source of common-sense intuitive solutions!)

Now I'll explain FREEZE-FRAME, a tool for intuitive perception, in more detail by giving a step-by-step example of how I've used it while dealing with upset and angry children and some of the benefits that resulted.*

---

*Editor's Note: A further explanation of this technique can be found in the book *FREEZE-FRAME: Fast Action Stress Relief.*

Step 1. Recognize the stressful feeling, and FREEZE-FRAME it. Take a time-out!

I'd just walked in the door from a marketing meeting and my mind was occupied with concerns about production delays and the backlog of orders to be filled. I was headed for the phone to find out the quantity of backorders, when I heard eight year old Josh and seven year old Blake yelling in the living room. A book came flying through the hallway. "I don't have time for this right now," I grumbled to myself and stomped into the living room. "What's going on? Who's throwing books around?," I barked impatiently. An angry cacophony of "He said, she said, no I didn't, yes you did," accosted my ears. Josh was the loudest so I told him to settle down. "But I didn't do it," he protested emphatically. "Why do I always get the blame?" "Everyone be quiet for a moment," I shouted over the din of voices. Josh would not listen to me and kept repeating shrilly, "But he started it, I didn't do anything." Then Blake yelled on top of Josh's protests, "Uh, uh, you did too, Josh, you grabbed the book from me first." The clamor and noise made it impossible to think. "I can't stand their constant bickering. It gets on my nerves. I'm not going to keep putting up with it," I thought to myself for the hundredth time. I could feel my blood pressure rising with each irritating thought, along with a feeling I was wasting time and needed to make that phone call. I realized I was in stress and decided to FREEZE-FRAME. Otherwise I would explode, send them to separate rooms, and still have to deal with them later. Taking a time-out in the middle of that racket wasn't my inclination, but I knew it would calm me down. So I did. That's Step 1: Recognize a stressful feeling, and FREEZE-FRAME it. Take a time-out!

Step 2. Make a sincere effort to shift your focus away from the racing mind or disturbed emotions to the area around your heart. Pretend you're breathing through your heart to help focus your energy in this area. Keep your focus there for ten seconds or more.

I stood there quietly observing for a moment, shifting my focus away from the kids and my impatient reactions to the area around my heart. I went to "neutral" and listened to myself breathing quietly through my heart for a few seconds, ignoring the tumult around me which was not getting any quieter. After about ten seconds, I could feel my heart rate slow down and I became calm. That was Step 2.

Step 3. Recall a positive fun feeling or time you've had in life and attempt to re-experience it.

Now that I was calm again, I went on to Step 3. I remembered it was just a week ago when the boys and I had gone on a golf cart ride through the hills and remembered the fun we'd had. I felt my love for them. They really were good kids, just a little wild at times. It had been raining for several days and they were restless indoors. As I stood there loving them, Josh came up to me and quietly asked with a little smile on his face, "What are you doing?" Blake looked up at me too. I didn't say anything. I went on to Step 4.

Step 4. Now, using your intuition, common sense, and sincerity — ask your heart — what would be a more efficient response to the situation, one that will minimize future stress?

I calmly asked my heart what would be a more effective way to handle these two, where they wouldn't quarrel as much, and I wouldn't get so irritated when they did. The boys had become silent as I stood there. Josh was fidgeting with the waist string on my jacket, while Blake went to retrieve the book from the hallway. With my emotions and mind calm, my heart feelings peaceful, I had the thought that this was really no big deal. The boys had been cooped up inside and didn't know what to do with themselves. At the same time, they needed to learn how to manage their restless energies on rainy days. I had a clear feeling just to talk to them calmly, share my perceptions, and listen to them.

Step 5. Listen to what your heart says in answer to your question.

So I sat down on the sofa and told them I understood it was hard to stay indoors in the rain. I asked them each to tell me, one at a time, and for the other to listen without talking, what they thought they could do differently so they wouldn't argue so much. Josh piped up, "There's nothing to do, except read, and he had the book I wanted." I reminded him that the question was, "What could you do differently?" Josh paused, then replied, "I could have asked if we could read it together." Then I asked Blake the same question. He replied, "I could have helped Josh find another book or maybe we could have found a game to play." I agreed those were good ideas and explained that grabbing someone else's book was not acceptable, even if you wanted it, nor was throwing books around acceptable behavior. The consequence would be they would both spend the next ten minutes straightening up the living room, putting their books, games, everything away. If they could do that quietly while I made a phone call, we would put on our boots and raincoats and do something fun after that. The boys agreed. I had fun planning a short adventure to the creek to see how much the rain had over-flowed the spillway. The phone call about the backorders was calmer than it would have been if this incident with the boys had not happened. My perspective expanded, not just with regards to the boys' need for some exercise, but my need to relax, check the spillway, get some exercise and explore too. We had fun and FREEZE-FRAME gave me the common-sense insight that accomplished several things at once. That was Step 5: Listen to what your heart says in answer to your question.

As you begin to experiment with FREEZE-FRAME, don't be discouraged if you don't remember to do it until after the fact. "After the fact" is better than not remembering at all. Many people will process negative thoughts and feelings for hours, days, weeks, months, and years. Freeze-Framing is about knowing how to shorten the duration of time you are consumed with all that undue stress. Shifting focus to the heart, and away from the problem, helps withdraw energy from the mind. Take a moment to relax in the heart. This allows you to consider more effective possibilities. The intelligence of pausing to take a deeper look before making choices is already inherent within the heart of each person. If you want to be the director of your own movie, you have to stop being just one of the characters and step back to see the whole picture.

FREEZE-FRAME is *very different* from "Stop and take a deep breath" or "Stop and count to 10." Count to 10 can be just the mind counting, which may not expand perception at all. That's why the intent of Freeze-Framing is to bring your energies to your heart and utilize the power of the heart. Recalling a positive episode or feeling assists you in seeing your current situation with more clarity and discernment. Re-experience a fun vacation, a meaningful relationship, a time in nature, a time with a child, a pet, etc. Remember how you **felt**. It's the positive feeling that activates the power of the heart and makes all the difference in being able to actualize your good intentions. Did you feel appreciation, care, compassion, or love in those grateful moments?

Sustaining a positive feeling can be difficult, especially if the situation you are Freeze-Framing is highly stressful and emotionally charged. The effort made to shift focus to a positive feeling, like appreciation, helps you *neutralize* the negative reactions. Becoming neutral in the face of stress is major progress. From neutral you have options on how to proceed. However, if you're unable to hold that objective position and find yourself again in the heat of things, don't give up. Be patient with yourself. Try to FREEZE-FRAME and find the neutral point again. *Neutral is a conduit for objectivity in the moment.*

Practicing FREEZE-FRAME is utilizing practical, preventive maintenance. Each time you try, you are building a positive behavior pattern. It's fun to see your personal stress deficit being reduced daily. As you practice Freeze-Framing, your own intuition, common sense, and sincerity become more active and available. This will increase your capacity to arrive at convenient and practical solutions.

Let's try it. Think of a current situation that's making you feel worried, anxious, frustrated, hopeless, etc. Go through the steps, one at a time, to find a new perspective that can reduce or prevent stress. If you act on what your heart intelligence tells you, you'll change the next scene in the movie of your reality. Try it out.

Sometimes it helps to write down your mental and emotional reactions to the situation (head reactions), then FREEZE-FRAME and write your heart intelligence response (heart perspective). The worksheet on the next page is an example.

Notice how different this mother's head and heart perceptions are. Freeze-Framing helps you distinguish the difference between your head and heart perceptions. Identify typical issues, times, situations, that are stressful to you. For example, many parents find mornings especially stressful. Everyone is rushing around getting ready for school, work, day care, arranging rides, meals, etc. If mornings are generally stressful, find a quiet time and do a FREEZE-FRAME to see what new perceptions and solutions your intuition can provide. The next morning try out what your heart intelligence tells you.

After attending IHM's "Empowered Parent®" seminar, Larry, a father of three teenage boys, decided to try Freeze-Framing to reduce the stress he was under most mornings. Here's his report. *"Mornings were the worst. The more I nagged my seventh grader to get up, get dressed, eat breakfast, and get to the bus stop on time, the more he seemed to dawdle. After Freeze-Framing, my intuition told me to speak only once, then let him deal with the consequences of missing his bus and having to walk to school. So the next morning, instead of my usual irritation and nagging, I gave him a hug, told him he had exactly twenty minutes to get ready and said nothing more. I was totally amazed when he was ready to go with five minutes to spare."*

Heart intuition brings a sense of security and knowingness about what to do. Try Freeze-Framing all situations that commonly cause you irritation or anxiety. There are many little everyday questions in parenting where Freeze-Framing can provide quick intuitive guidance, like whether to send a child to day care if he's coming down with a cold, what age to let him stay home alone, whether to let your child buy a particular toy, eat a sweet snack, play with a troublesome friend, and many others. Practice FREEZE-FRAME to improve your common sense — the intuitional capacity. It creates a joyous sense of freedom.

INSTITUTE OF HEARTMATH®

FREEZE-FRAME® WORKSHEET

STEPS:

1. STRESSFUL SITUATION: Write down a few words that describe the situation.
2. HEAD REACTION: Write down how you have been mentally or emotionally reacting to this situation.
3. FREEZE-FRAME: Take a time-out!
4. SHIFT TO THE HEART: Focus your attention in the area around the heart for 20 to 30 seconds.
5. ACTIVATE A HEART FEELING: Recall a positive experience or feel care or appreciation for someone or something.
6. ACCESS HEART PERSPECTIVE: Use your intuition, common sense, and sincerity to determine what would be a more efficient response to the situation and write it down.

STRESSFUL SITUATION   *My 2 kids argue and fight constantly.*

HEAD REACTION   *I get frustrated, feel guilty, lose my temper, feel inadequate, get impatient, blame myself and then worry. Suppertime is stressful. I blame my husband for not helping.*

FREEZE-FRAME

HEART PERSPECTIVE   *Set clear rules about arguing and fighting, and clear consequences — stick to them. Use Freeze-Frame in the moment to keep myself calm. My anger is sometimes from feeling we don't spend enough quality time together. We're always rushing. So schedule quality time as a family. Take a walk together, plan something fun for the evening. Organize myself better.*

How Children Relate To FREEZE-FRAME

Children naturally shift feelings faster than adults. This is because children are less subject to non-efficient mind-sets and therefore are more flexible. Teaching children a character-building tool like FREEZE-FRAME helps them retain their flexibility. They learn how to release negative feelings quickly and activate their heart intuition. A child who practices Freeze-Framing when feeling hurt, worried, upset, or stressed gains self-empowerment. He learns to tell himself in effect, "Wait a minute, I'm stuck, I'm in a head jam, my emotions are going out of control, slow down, find the heart, perceive the consequences — I need to FREEZE-FRAME!" Inner silence feels fulfilling even to a child. Common sense and intuitive heart understanding will then tell him what to do. Self-esteem builds as the choices a child makes consistently result in feeling good later. (To understand how to teach children the FREEZE-FRAME tool, please refer to Chapter 9.)

Through practicing FREEZE-FRAME, children learn for themselves that each choice has a consequence. When they have this heart-intelligent understanding, they are prepared to proceed with self-empowerment.

Here's what ten year old Keith said he discovered through FREEZE-FRAME practice: *"I almost joined a gang without knowing it. The gang was kids from age ten to fourteen, about forty to fifty kids. I knew the leader. We were sort of friends. I would get in trouble a lot at school. They look for kids in trouble. I could defend myself pretty well, too. This gang guy, his parents abuse him. He goes around scaring kids and doesn't realize what he's doing. That's where HeartMath stepped in. Lock-ins — you go to your heart and you stay there. You then feel good about today and what you're going to do. It taught me a lot. FREEZE-FRAME and staying in my heart. Normally I would flip out and lose it. There goes my brain and I'm possessed. Anybody want to fight, come on, I'm ready! Now, instead of looking for fights, I avoid them. I FREEZE-FRAME as hard as I can. What's done is done, let it go. I didn't think it would work but it does. Everybody has power in their heart. Some people just don't bother to use it."*

Chapter 4

Managing And Improving Your Mind

The brain, mind, and intellect operate concurrently on frequencies which are different from heart frequencies. That's why I refer to the brain/mind/intellect collectively as "the head." The primary duty of the head is to sort, process, and analyze information. This is an important role. It's vital for reading, writing, thinking, and talking. However, if not balanced with heart wisdom, the head is capable of independently generating feelings, plans, and projections of its own. The head leans toward thinking about what's suitable only for itself and focusing on negative perspectives. Hatred, revenge, envy, condescension, greed, arrogance, self-pity, insecurity, and many more feelings come from attitudes spawned by the head. These attitudes, reinforced over time, can create an unseen cloud of mental and emotional impurities. This continues to magnetize still more detrimental thoughts and attitudes. People become victimized by this ongoing process within them. These mental attitudes and thoughts are by-products of comparison, assessment, or analysis. The unmanaged head, functioning without the intuitive intelligence of the heart, propagates distorted and stressful perspectives. Heart intelligence is what maximizes the brain's highest potential. The brain can't do it by itself.

Mind Processing

Have you ever noticed how quickly the mind works? Someone can say half a sentence and we've already decided this is going to be a drag, a chore, unfair, or boring. Or, we've gone sailing into imagination or memory — projecting what it might be like or finding associations with what's been said. Children do this often. All I have to say to an eight year old I know is, "That toy you have is . . . " and he'll interrupt with a lengthy description of how it's the best toy, his mom got it for him, it's better than his friend's, and on and on.

Most people speak at a rate of 120-150 words per minute, but *the thinking process is five to eight times faster than the rate of speech.* Because of the speed of the thinking process, it is easy to make snap judgments, have quick opinions, and suffer random head chatter and mechanical thought processes, frequently without being aware of it. Thoughts run rampant a lot of the time. How often have you had the experience where thoughts just won't shut off? They repeat like an old LP record stuck in a groove. Children acquire such mind patterns from the adults around them.

My comments about head intelligence are not intended to diminish the incredible potential of the brain but to show what is required to enhance it. Each of our brain's ten billion neurons (nerve cells) contains a sophisticated information programming system. Each neuron is a processing hub, capable in an instant of deliberating thousands of competing signals and evaluating how to respond to them. What we call "experience" occurs through the exchange of frequencies of information between neurons and surrounding force fields.[7] Neurons don't hold information any more than the transistors and tubes of a radio or TV contain the show they play. Is it really the neuron — that combination of cold and indifferent chemicals — that permits a human being to not just physically see, but to perceive? Perception is more than just the physical image you are *seeing*. It is also the *feeling*.

I remember watching a seven year old girl playing house, pretending she was the mama and her doll was the baby. She sounded exactly like her mother, worried and anxious, telling the doll at least three times, "Now, put on your sweater before you go outside," then interrupting herself with, "But Mommy, I'm not cold." She began nagging the doll with one objection after another. Children's play often mimics adult behavior. By the time they're teenagers, these learned behavior patterns become more set. They become *mind-sets.*

Teenagers talk on the phone to each other saying the same thing over and over: "Dude man," or "No way man," or worrying out loud, "If I dress that way, they'll think I'm not cool," "None of the other kids do," "It's not fair . . . ," just like one of those songs on the radio. As habitual mental patterns become etched in the brain, many teens and adults find they often can't shut off their mind and relax. Or they can't sleep at night because of the daytime chatter still running wild. Physical addictions to alcohol, drugs, etc., often result from the understandable urge to escape ongoing, unfulfilling thought patterns. These addictive thoughts become imprisoning realities that we are creating, resulting in stress and wear and tear on the human body. They never bring peace of mind. Addictive thought patterns also block further development of the brain's pre-frontal cortex, which is associated with more compassionate human intelligence and behavior.

Judgments

Judgments transpire mid-thought, mid-sentence, unforeseen, unplanned. Knowingly or unknowingly, many people suffer judgmental patterns. Daily, hundreds of internal judgmental thoughts and feelings just happen; they are a commonplace occurrence in life. If you habitually judge other people, places or things, you are modeling that approach to life for your children. Judgments sneak in, so guard against these speculations and emotional lawsuits against others. Continuous criticizing and judging are what isolate people from meaningful heart relationships. Judgments stop real communication and halt heart-to-heart talks.

Recall an occasion when you judged someone. How did it feel? When I judged someone I loved because she didn't live up to my expectations, I felt pained and cut off from her and thought it was her fault. The pain didn't cease until I made peace with her. Emotional judgments can be tough to unchain. Each effort to unleash a judgment is an instrumental step toward having peace within.

Often people are their own worst critics. They've been taught that being self-critical is an asset, unaware of how they are hurting themselves through negative self-judgment. Parents repeatedly stress themselves as they think: "I'm not a good enough parent" or "Where did I go wrong?" For example, if you assess that your son has a "personality oddity" or behavior problem, you might ask yourself where you went wrong, become emotional, and judge yourself until you're despondent. Seven year old Gary was still wetting his bed at night. His frustrated mother tried every remedy she could find. The doctor tried to reassure her that Gary would outgrow the habit, yet the distraught mother was sure she must have done something wrong and blamed herself for not creating a good enough environment. When faced with challenges, parents need to see how they might do better, but judging themselves won't help. Never-ending self-judgments forestall us from seeing ourselves and our children realistically. They make knowing what and how to change impossible. To find new solutions and hope, see if you can love more. Slow down, practice a HEART LOCK-IN each day and send love to yourself and your child. Practice staying in your heart perceptions as you relate to your child and let new intuitive insights come to you.

If there is any one circumstance guaranteed to stop real intuition, it's self-judgment. Self-judging blocks intuitive clarity and rules out utilization of our talents and energies in an enhancing way. Prosperity occurs from acknowledgment and appreciation of our own skills and talents. Honorably undertake a sincere effort to be all that you can be. Judgments breed hatred, blame and envy, which don't establish a secure self. A sixteen year old girl I recently read about was a good student and well-liked, but envious of her fifteen year old sister's greater popularity and many boyfriends. She was so mentally preoccupied with jealousy that she undermined her own self worth, her grades began to slip, and she developed an eating disorder.

What is the difference between judgment and assessment? Seeing this distinction is of utmost importance. When forming an assessment about your own or someone else's actions, beliefs, or appearances and a rush of negative thoughts and emotional feeling occurs — this is a judgment, an unproductive act. Judgments are negative comparisons, often between ourselves and another person. When comparisons are based on insecurities, they delude our perceptions. Children are frequently assessed and compared in society, then judgmentally labeled and categorized. A child is likely to brush off those judgments casually if the chief people in his life have loved and supported him. Assessments brought about *without* heart keenness are what beget judgments and produce stress.

Exercising assessment and containing one's conduct require the ability to foresee the future consequences of one's current behavior. Children and adults need to make assessments to discover what's real in life. Heart intelligence presents to children and adults the skills to assess a situation and consider it with common sense. Assessing oneself is beneficial and precedes honest self-adjustment. An associate told me when she was eight years old she realized that she cried at least four times a week and wished she could stop. She locked herself in the privacy of the bathroom to figure out why. She assessed that each incident was related to her brothers' picking on her. She'd get mad, then when they wouldn't stop she'd blame them, feel helpless, and cry. She decided to make an effort not to let them get to her and not to cry the next time. This is heart intelligence in action.

Blame

Unmanaged head reactions and judgments often feel justified. Someone does something that we don't like or agree with, so we feel hurt and blame them. If a child gives a cookie to one friend but not to another, the child who didn't get the cookie feels left out, blames the other child, calls him "a stupid dummy." The head says, "It's obvious it's his fault because his actions hurt me." We all know how that feels. The head holds on and can't see any options. The child's intellect can't understand. But the child's heart knows to let it go and before long the two children will probably be playing happily again.

Blaming usually implies that we do not take responsibility for our own perceptions, feelings, words, or actions. If we think blame, the underlying feelings and stress often create negative expressions or emotionally-charged word framings. Whether it's a disgusted look, a cold shoulder, or accusing words, a lack of heart is conveyed. It is simple to perceive how a child could feel that his actions that led to these negative expressions are synonymous with his value as a person. As parents learn to get their points across from a sincere business-like heart, instead of with blaming looks and words, they will find their children more responsive. Here's an example: Six year old Daniel kept interrupting the guests' conversations during his mother's bridge club. He ignored constant reminders to wait until people were through talking. His demands for attention were an irritant to all. A head-reaction mom screams and focuses the blame on Daniel, "You are a bad boy. You are rude and thoughtless!" Or she twists the blame into a question, "Don't you care about anyone?" "Don't you have any respect?" Negative phrases, "bad boy," "rude," "thoughtless," or questioning his care or respect, bash her son's self-worth. The head-reaction mom reacts too quickly to her disturbed perceptions and feelings. She is not taking responsibility for her own embarrassment and transfers the blame to her son. If she would calm down, ask her bridge partners to wait one minute, stop and listen to her child, then she could help him hush. She would engage heart intelligence to deal with the undercurrents of her head reaction feelings and her child's behavior.

A heart-reaction mom responds to the situation differently from the start. She FREEZE-FRAMES to gather her emotions, find a heart perception, and frame her response to the situation. She articulates her reaction to her son's conduct by clearly expressing her own feelings with words such as, "I'm tired of all these interruptions," "I don't want to keep telling you to be quiet," or "I'm irritated that you don't listen to me." The heart-reaction mom *communicates feelings without blame.* How you talk to children helps them determine the essential difference between feelings, actions, and self-worth.

Negative judgments cause a child to feel less acceptable as a person. When a child's self-valuation is conditional upon performance, the joyous spirit is likely to withdraw. A child whose father did well academically can feel pressured to do the same. A father who judges his daughter's C grades, then compares them to his own grades as a child, thinks he is helping when he states, "As a student I made A's. Why can't you? Are you stupid? You're not trying!" The child feels like a failure. The child can also feel if she does not achieve, she will not be loved. Furthermore, showing judgmental patterns to children teaches them that they also have the freedom to judge. Thus, children can justify head reactions to their surroundings rather than heart perceiving. The daughter whom dad is judging for not achieving higher grades feels she has the right to judge her younger brother for not doing things right. As he falters trying to learn to ride a bike, she calls him stupid. Judgmentalness doesn't institute a constructive atmosphere for anyone.

Parents can't always see what effects their judgmental reactions or their stress have on a child. Let's use another example to illustrate: A stressed father just arrived home from a pressure-filled day at work and can't find the remote control to the TV. Short-tempered, he yells at his young son to "go find that remote," assuming the boy has left it somewhere. The child cringes. If he did misplace the remote, he feels his father sees him as incompetent. If he did not misplace it, he perceives that he must have done something wrong to incur his dad's wrath. The father is finding fault with him and holding him responsible, so the boy self-blames. Not knowing his father is under stress, he doesn't understand.

The image parents project to children is a principal means youngsters use to view themselves as competent or incompetent. When a parent is under stress, the image they project is distorted and not what their true heart would intend. With all the conflicting demands of life today, parenting is simply more stressful. The family interrelationships of today's American society are unparalleled in history — single parents, step-parents, and foster parents are increasingly common.

For numerous children, parenting is performed solely by one biological mother who works full-time.

Between 1970 and 1994 there was a 200% growth rate in single-parent households, from 4 million to 8 million homes.

The divorce rate remains at 50%. Each year over 1,000,000 children are newly affected. One-third of these children will never see one of their parents again.

In situations of divorce, it is estimated that a child internalizes the stress and anger between the parents 60% of the time, truly believing, "It's all my fault," and feels rejected by at least one parent. In addition to a divorced parent having less time to spend with children, the repercussions of divorce include greater financial burden, added stress, and growing numbers of problem children. But a parent's self-blame is never an answer to any of these problems.

Overcoming Judgments

Parents who perceive from an understanding heart observe their own and their children's stresses honestly and sincerely. They frequently ask themselves, "How do I speak the real truth?" "How do I inspire my child to listen?" They realize that judgmental statements only invite children to defend themselves or to tune parents out.

It is possible to speak the truth without judgments. Your heart intelligence can show you how. Before communicating with your child, first do a HEART LOCK-IN and radiate love for your child. Focus in the heart, then ask your intuitive intelligence, "How do I cease accusations and communicate without using judgments?" In the earlier example of the father who was disappointed with his daughter's C grades, the father's intuition might tell him, "First ask Jenny the reason she thinks her grades are low. Then, after listening to her perceptions, speak the truth of my own perceptions." His intuition might also say, "Radiate heart to her. It could change her disposition or uncover solutions as we communicate." When parents love, children are more apt to communicate their real feelings. As Jenny feels understood and helped by dad, she will have more patience and understanding with her little brother Joe as he tries to ride his bike.

Attaining awareness of "judgmentalness" will not remove decades of habit overnight. But love and care will shave the edges off judgment and blame, then dissipate them entirely within time. Be sure not to judge yourself for having been judgmental. That's just more of the same. Grab a tool instead.

Practice the HEART LOCK-IN and FREEZE-FRAME tools provided in this manual. The HEART LOCK-IN will help you perceive that one's assessments and feelings are an individual's truth in that moment. They are not good or bad value judgments. By practicing FREEZE-FRAME during stressful moments, your heart intelligence will release judgmental reaction patterns and provide deeper perception and understanding. Heart perception, intelligence, and practice can transform any parent or child.

Chapter 5

The Impact of Stress

I was talking to a divorced mother, Coreen, who has two boys, ages eight and fourteen. She was telling me how difficult it is to combine career and child-rearing: *"My boss expects me to work fifty to sixty hours a week if I want to climb in the ranks, get a raise, or even hold onto my job. My kids make their own breakfasts every day and suppers at least four times a week. I know I'm going to burn out if things don't change, and my doctor has just given me a stronger prescription for my ulcer."*

Coreen also told me she struggles with guilt about the kids, about her desire for a mate with no time to date, and about her future. She can only afford a housekeeper once a week, the TV has become a convenient baby-sitter, and her teenager never talks to her anymore. As we talked, Coreen let me know that her next door neighbors, Alysse and her husband Don, also find raising children to be very stressful. Both parents commute over one hour to work in heavy traffic to earn enough to support three kids, a hefty mortgage, and two car payments. Polls show that together, Coreen and Alysse represent over 25 million American households where parents report they have no time to spend with their children.

Graham Burrows, M.D., Professor of Psychiatry and President of the International Society for the Investigation of Stress reported, "There are two main factors underlying stress: Problems in perception and problems in communication . . . There is a need to adopt preventive rather than curative strategies."[11] Stress is an internal feedback signal indicating inharmonious or uncomfortable feelings. We've all experienced uncomfortable feelings. Where do they come from? How do we perceive them? How do we deal with them? Stressful feelings result from our non-effective mental and emotional reactions to events in life. Do you as a parent have the knowledge and know-how to deal with stress? How did Coreen handle her stress before she began to practice HeartMath? Coreen relayed the following story:

"I spent a long hard day at the office, then took a trip to the grocery store on the way home. As I walked into the kitchen, I saw garbage spilling over. So I shouted to my fourteen year old, 'Steven, why haven't you taken out the garbage?' Steven just sneered at me and said, 'I don't have time, I have to do my homework and you never do anything anymore.' Well my blood boiled. He pushed my most sensitive button. I got really angry and told him, 'I'm trying to take care of you and your brother. At least you could do your chores.' Steven smashed his history book on the table, ran to his bedroom and slammed the door — totally ignoring me and the garbage. I just lost it and screamed through the door, 'You are so ungrateful!' I know Steve wants to move out and go live with a friend. I heard him say it on the phone when he didn't know I was listening. He never tells me anything.

"So then I had to tackle the pile of bills and mail on the table. Next to the pile I found a crumpled note that Mark, my eight year old, had brought from school saying he got into a fight again and I needed to be at the principal's office at 10:00 a.m. the next day. I was so drained and stressed-out, I just poured myself a drink and slumped down on the sofa. It was just too much to handle."

Steven is just one of 97% of teenagers in a 1994 *New York Times /*

CBS News survey who said they are afraid to tell their parents what they really do or think. Coreen is just one of 53% of parents polled from all socio-economic groups in a 1991 *L.A. Times* survey who gave themselves poor marks on child-rearing, admitting they don't do a good job guiding their children. They also feel their kids are undisciplined and lack morals, and they feel frustrated and guilty not knowing how to help their children.

While parents struggle with their stresses, a child's little body and intelligence struggle to deal with life's challenges and then respond accordingly. According to internationally acclaimed British child psychiatrist and researcher, Michael Rutter, "Children learn problem-solving mostly from seeing how their parents and other adults deal with things." It's no wonder children are having difficulty coping. Without learning skills to effectively reduce stress, the constant accumulation of little stresses will build into chronic stress.

A human system grows in balance by learning how to deal with the challenging ups and downs or waves of life. Challenges approached from the heart actually build creative resistance and resiliency. Each new recognition and successful adaptation to life's events allows a child to move assuredly into unknown experiences. Heart understanding builds the confidence to master each new challenge.

When parents are in strong disagreement with each other's perspectives, it creates confusion and compounds stress for their child. A mother of a seven year old boy, Paul, relayed the following: *"I was in the midst of very hostile relations with my ex-husband. He was extremely angry with me for the divorce, and although he cooperated on child visitation, he was rigid and inflexible with agreed-upon time schedules. We both lived in Chicago and relied upon the city's usually excellent public transportation. I had my son for the day, and we were at the bus stop in freezing weather, waiting for the bus so I could escort him back to his father's. We waited and waited . . . due to whatever reasons, the bus was very late so I was late returning my son to his father's care. I was freezing, stressed out, upset. There was nothing I could do — not even make a phone call explaining the situation. I did my best to hide these feelings from my child. When we arrived at my ex-husband's, he was furious and yelled at me. He gave me no opening for any explanation. Our son burst into tears. His stress was that his parents hated each other and treated each other so terribly — and with regards to him. Paul ran into his room, isolated and upset. My ex slammed the door on me. I felt deep, heart-wrenching stress."* Do you think Paul has the knowledge or know-how to deal with this stressful challenge?

If a child's life events are continuously non-productive, challenges become overwhelming stressors. A child's perception then renders a feeling of instability. Parents seem unreliable and life is scary, creating heightened stress that leads to critical damage. The child does not know how to adapt. So for survival, he withdraws and blocks out reality itself.

A Stress Epidemic

Stress has no regard for rich or poor, educated or uneducated. Wealthy socialites, factory workers, people on welfare, and nuclear physicists all have stress today. Chronic stress is a disease and dysfunction of our disturbed society. While life has always had violence, abuse, and stressful periods, chronic stress is a new epidemic of modern society.

Nationwide, millions of children each year are emotionally and physically abused or neglected. Family violence and stressful disruptions at home have been shown to prevent infants and young children from developing normal sleeping and eating patterns so they fail to thrive. Richard Gelles, of the University of Rhode Island's Family Violence Research Program, found that young children who witness family violence often become non-verbal, depressed, lethargic, almost autistic. They have terrible nightmares. They strike themselves. They become desensitized by constant low levels of violence. Children raised in abusive homes are two to three times more likely to grow up to be violent adults.

Violence shows children that parents and society do not value life. Polls reveal that from the inner city to affluent neighborhoods, children's major source of stress and concern is fear of violence. Over 50% say they fear walking near their homes in the dark. Regardless of where they live, students see violence as so vast and complex that few have any confidence in the ability of adults to solve it. Over 80% of youngsters expect the problems to keep going from bad to worse.

Fear of physical violence is only one cause of high stress. Emotional blackmail, such as not talking to a spouse or child for weeks out of anger, banging dishes to show unhappiness, or stony silence at the dinner table each night, can also cause tremendous stress. Without a safe place to be, no energy can be utilized for exploring potentials or knowing fulfillment, so the chronic stress generates more fears. Children spend the rest of their lives trying to escape these fears in search of security.

It's clear that the absence of heart intelligence causes a cluster of problems for children and adults, regardless of where they live or their background. Stress reduces intelligence and perspective, which makes it harder to deal with existing challenges and problems. A 1989 Harris poll revealed that nearly 90% of all adults in the U.S. say they experience high levels of stress. According to a Northwestern National Life Insurance survey, one in three Americans seriously thought of quitting work in 1990 because of job stress, and one in three expected to "burn out" on the job in the near future. Seven of the top ten selling prescription drugs in the U.S. are for stress-related complaints, such as ulcers, hypertension, depression, and anxiety. If these statistics reflect how adults are dealing with life, then how are children supposed to do better? When parents are this stressed out, they are probably caught in a vicious circle with their own life and children. Children, in turn, are caught in a web of their own perceptions and reactions to a parent's stressed and busy life.

What's a Parent to Do?

A child's misbehavior often sets up a fierce sequence of negative parental reaction, as in Coreen's situation. It can begin with a nagging contest to get your child to clean up after himself or do the simplest chores. He may lose TV privileges and his allowance, be sent to his room or grounded for days, yet nothing improves. At this point, I wonder how many times an exasperated parent has thought or said, "What do I do?" A few years later, there may be verbal, screaming battles regarding homework, grades, curfews, or use of the car. Some children lie, swear, put on headphones to listen to heavy metal or rap and won't talk. The difficulties can mount into full scale war if a parent finds out her teenager is stealing money from her wallet, experimenting with drugs, having sex, or planning to run away.

Continuous stress and hardships do cause problematic conduct in children and teenagers. Parents try to cope with these toilsome issues but get poor results. As the power duels escalate between parent and child, discipline is less and less effective. You want the child to do something and the child won't. The child won't even listen so the parent gets frustrated and furious. In Coreen's situation, she descended to Steven's level, head reaction yelling, then slamming the door on the problems. If continued, Steven will no longer perceive Coreen as the parental authority figure.

When parental authority is lost, the parent is totally at a loss, not knowing what to do. A lack of understanding, as well as being worn out, can compound fears, guilt, and anxieties. Coreen could feel as though she is at a point of no return. If this is true in your home, I can understand why you may feel no hope and wonder where you went wrong. If you feel like Coreen, Alysse and Don, or millions of other frustrated parents, now is a good time to take a deep breath, bring the energy to your heart, relax, find peace of mind, and realize you sincerely love your child. Coreen did find new hope in practicing the tools provided in this manual. She says, *"The tools have been a godsend. I don't always remember to use them, but when I do, they work. I don't yell at the boys as much and we are actually talking now."* So, continue reading to understand the deeper causes underlying these problems and find out what to do.

A Choice

A key HeartMath principle in dealing with parent/child combat consists of individuals understanding how their perceptions, thoughts, choices, and actions condition the events and outcomes of their lives. If not taught heart values at home, children repeatedly make ineffective choices and learn through tough experiences. Again and again this shatters them, leaving them with a "there is nothing we can do about it" attitude. It is crucial for parents to remember that perception is the passport to knowing how a child sees, chooses, and acts. A heart intelligent parent penetrates a child's world not to agree or disagree, but to *understand without judgment.* Practicing the Freeze-Framing tool will assist you in developing sincere communication, deeply listening, and speaking your truth to yourself and your children.

Sheila and Bill were having trouble with Linda, their twelve year old daughter, who was lying to them. Sheila Freeze-Framed, went to her heart and got a clear perception that showed her she had not really been listening to her daughter. She decided to spend more time with Linda and listen without reacting to whatever Linda said. Bill, on the other hand, stonewalled his daughter. His head told him she was ungrateful and lied once too often. He wrote her off.

Two different perspectives of the same situation. It's a matter of the heart or head choice in how we deal with problems. The heart choice offers a possible opportunity for solutions. The head choice imprisons us in hurt or anger.

Head Choices

When people perceive from the *head*, they react to life in a variety of ways: Continuously failing to find solutions, success, or happiness, they can become depressed. Linda's father, Bill, feels like life is against him. He's been out of work and depressed. His daughter's behavior makes him feel more of a failure. Depressed people often perceive that they don't have the capability to help their situation, so they *surrender their happiness*. They feel uncertain, unsafe, and fearful.

When a problem child's behavior is puzzling, parents responding from the head become immensely uncertain of their responses. They simply don't know what's going on inside the child, therefore they cannot construct consistent solutions. A mother who can't control her child feels the child is unresponsive and laborious to raise. Mothers in this situation project that no one understands. They feel hopeless. Many withdraw from their relationships. Their sex life dwindles. Divorce is common. Some turn to alcohol or create "other lives" away from their families for escape. Others turn to violence.

Increasing numbers of problem children also turn to violence; their fearful parents search desperately for reasons why. Ralph, whose teenage son was caught by police stealing the family car and having sex with a junior high school girl, blamed himself for being a poor father. Although in his wife's eyes he had been a good father, he still felt tremendous guilt, believing if only he'd done something differently he could have prevented the situation. As I said earlier, self-blame is a judgmental head reaction that has never helped anyone solve anything. If not curbed, self-blame and guilt eventuate in depression.

Millions resort to crime or violence to gain a sense of power. The selfish head says, "Get what you can now," with little concern for others or the consequences. Many who operate largely from head reactions are competitive, overly ambitious, argumentative, highly critical and even insulting. But they often pay the price in broken relationships and ill health.

People also use the threat of gang warfare, terrorist attacks, earthquakes, economic uncertainties, homelessness, or AIDS as an excuse to view life from the head. In their fear they feel there is nothing that can change this stark reality, so they just resign. Yet, each generation has faced its own threats. In the frontier days, diseases such as tuberculosis and cholera could rapidly destroy entire communities. In the Civil War days, there was no assurance that the men would return home from the battle. Head reactions are not new. There are just new pressures and threats today. Fulfillment or the lack of it does not depend predominantly on events and elements external to yourself. *It depends on internal attitudes and perspectives.*

Expectation is another common head reaction which sets people up for disappointment and stress. You care, so you expect your child to behave a certain way. But if you have an emotional investment in that expectation, you will be disappointed if she doesn't act accordingly. As you start feeling sympathy for yourself, you justify "your right" to feel hurt, worried, or sad. If unchecked, sympathy will drain your energy and you'll find yourself in a state of *"poor-me."* Hopelessness or fear of the future come from not being able to perceive life through the heart. Understand again that you have two basic choices — the head or the heart. One victimizes, the other empowers.

Heart Choices

Here are some typical characteristics of people who consistently respond to life from the *heart.* While not perfect, they have a higher ratio of the following qualities: Their decisions and actions are based on heart perceptions. They feel secure — a security that has been built from seeing the effective results of decisions based on heart perceptions. They listen to the hearts of others and to their own hearts to find intuitive perspectives. When there are circumstances they cannot change, they still use their hearts to decide how best to respond.

Parents of children with difficult natures frequently feel they are not managing adequately. Having to excessively govern a child demands a lot of chasing, cleaning up, and is unquestionably exhausting. Anger is a common result. But parents who stop and listen to their intuitive intelligence feel there is always a way to understand and find answers to problems. They know life is constantly changing and that lasting security can come only from within their own heart. They possess a genuine care for the whole and heart sensitivity to all that transpires. Even amid the challenges, their relationships blossom. People who view life from the heart increasingly realize that prosperity and health originate from within themselves; they feel successful and happy.

If you have a difficult child or one that's going through a difficult period, self-forgiveness and forgiving your child are vital heart choices. Realize that you and your child are each doing the best you know how. If you've tried to forgive but resentments resurface, don't look at yourself as a failure. Be seriously sincere with yourself and remember the importance of forgiveness. Practice FREEZE-FRAME, go back to your heart intelligence, listen for your inner wisdom and *feel* forgiveness — for yourself, your child, other family members, teachers, society. Do it over and over again until you feel free. You can do it. Through compassion, love, and intuitive understanding, a parent can discover new possibilities to make a situation workable.

Compassion

Compassion is an effective antidote for head reactions that generate fear, expectation, and "poor-me." Compassion is ignited when we realize that each person (including yourself) is unique, then connect in the heart at the essence level and desire to understand that person's being. When you care and have passion to understand, you become compassionate.

It is important to have balance in your compassion. People are susceptible to feelings of compassion slipping into sympathy due to emotional over-identity. Over-identifying with a child's difficulties is extremely draining, entangling you in your child's problems, stimulating over-protectiveness of his needs, and blocking your ability to clearly perceive. Balanced compassion sustains heart perception and empowers creative solutions.

Transforming Repression

One of the greatest blocks to the flow of heart perception is repression. When negative feelings stack and are repressed, the body stays in a state of stress. As pressures build, release occurs through various exits — nail-biting, hair twisting, over-sensitivity, hyperactivity, and psychosomatic ailments. Continuous internal turbulence pilots chronic fatigue and downgrades resistance to physical disease. Energies in repression are not accessible for constructive use. Repression doesn't merely bury negative emotions, it inhibits warm-hearted emotions as well.

An example is when children share emotions with us, adults classically dictate how they should be feeling instead. This leads to repression. Parent, put yourself in your child's shoes to perceive how such dictates would challenge you. Imagine yourself as a seven year old bawling because your puppy died and your parents say, "It's only a dog. You shouldn't cry over an animal. Big kids don't cry." How does this sound to a child whose puppy was his best friend to confide in, cuddle, and love? This is an extreme example, but the search for heart understanding is what motivates any child to open up about his real feelings and find release.

Heart understanding creates an allowance and acceptance of feelings. Comprehending your negative feelings transfers the emotions into frames of understanding, so you escape repression. HeartMath tools help people acknowledge, understand, and release repressed feelings. Educate a child to know she is worthy and valued because of her feelings. Her feelings are what enable her to accept the humanness of others. Releasing feelings lifts children so they perceive their problems realistically rather than fallaciously. It reforms the entire system as one achieves self-assurance. Children construct this inner assurance by trusting in the heart. Self-esteem is the developed essence of heart power. Complete self-esteem is built from structured heart empowerment — having the heart and the "math" to fix what's broken.

In researching the nature of the heart and self-empowerment at IHM, we scientifically discovered which perspectives are empowering and lead to balance and fulfillment, and which are depleting and lead to stress. As parents choose empowering perspectives about life, children will follow. When Skyler, a twelve year old who attends IHM's Kid Care Program, was asked, "How do you feel about life?" and "How do you think other kids feel?" he answered: *"Life is an adventure and it is a challenge. One day could be a bad day, a challenge, and the next day could be an adventure, like taking a field trip to the woods. I'm glad I'm alive. Some kids are depressed, some are happy. Life changes. Whatever comes forward affects you. When I was a little kid, I'd get in trouble. And then I started changing. I was tired of being grumpy and mad at people! People can change because if they look at their life and what they don't like, they can make a choice to change it."*

There is hope for the family, and that hope is sustained as you practice using your heart. As you learn to access heart intelligence *consciously and consistently,* you'll secure wiser, more productive choices in all facets of your life. Have patience with yourself and your children as you implement these principles and tools. Parents and children aren't perfect people. Don't become discouraged if your child has a bad week or if you lose it one day and find yourself stressed-out and screaming at your child. Effective self-management and uncovering heart empowerment deserve a little practice.

Chapter 6

How to Care
Without Overcare

Once you've learned to go to neutral and access your heart intelligence with FREEZE-FRAME, then you can begin to discriminate balanced care within yourself. Webster's Dictionary definition of "care" is consistent with how millions of parents think about care. In the dictionary, "care" is first described as a troubled or burdensome state of mind, worry, concern. Why is this, when people also think of care as a wonderful, nurturing feeling? An example of the dictionary type of "care" is a parent fretting and crying miserably over a child who has stayed out past the parent's curfew. When the nurturing feeling of care turns into worry and stress, it becomes "overcare."

Overcare is debilitating for all concerned. A parent's unceasing overcare fuels a child's frustration, anxiety, and anguish. Parents who overcare put their own limiting perceptions onto children. They nag, often without knowing if what they are demanding is in the child's best interests. They worry constantly about their children, thinking they are actually caring about them. In reality, children recoil from parents who are forever correcting and worrying them. *Overcare draws misery* while making people think it's a means of preventing misery. Releasing overcare starts with acknowledging that the correct cause (your genuine care) was merely annexed to stressful mental processing, such as worry, fretting, distress, or grief.

How do parents know if they are caring or overcaring? Ask yourself, *"Is my care stress-producing or stress-reducing?"* Overcare produces stress. Balanced care is stress-reducing and productive. Use FREEZE-FRAME to distinguish the difference in yourself. Realize that any uncomfortable feeling, from a subtle feeling of unease to an obvious feeling of worry, anxiety, insecurity, fear, anguish, regret, guilt, etc., is overcare. It is your mind that has taken your genuine care to inefficient extremes. Parental overcare perpetuates insecurity and energy drain — all in the name of care. I address overcare in depth in my book *CUT-THRU: Achieve Total Security and Maximum Energy, A Scientifically Proven Insight on How to Care Without Becoming a Victim.* In this *Parenting Manual* I will discuss overcare specifically as it relates to parenting.

Check yourself for overcare:

☐ Do you find yourself worrying about your child?

☐ Do you fret about your child's attitudes, habits, friends, or school?

☐ Are you troubled that your child is undisciplined or lacks morals?

☐ Do you feel strain or affliction in trying to care for your child, along with work, household, other family members, etc.?

☐ Are you frustrated by a lack of time to spend with your child?

☐ Do you feel guilty or regret how you have treated your child?

☐ Are you dismayed that you don't know how to help your child feel more loved, accepted, or important?

☐ Do you feel anxiety or alarm about your child's future?

Parents attending IHM Empowered Parenting Retreats identified the following areas of their parental overcare. See if any of these apply to you or parents you know.

- Overexplaining everything, wanting to make sure my child "gets it," wanting him to understand so I nag or lecture, yet I still can't "get through" to him.

- Too often planning and making decisions for my children. Trying to be a savior, instead of a dad.

- Worry makes me ask too many questions to try to find out what's going on.

- Nagging him about manners, being polite, social appearance.

- Guilty about time for myself and enough time with my kids.

- Overcare about not making waves or causing conflicts with my kids.

Overcare arises from insecurity, yet overcare never resolves the insecurity. Balanced care arises from a feeling of security and creates more security. As parents learn not to *overcare* but find *balanced care,* they build a stronger intuitive connection with their child. Overcare can cut the intuitive connection and run a child off. Often children prefer to leave home and love from a distance rather than have to deal with an overcaring parent. As kids are repelled from parental overcare, the typical parental reaction is to try harder and harder.

A prominent executive who visited IHM told me he didn't understand overcare. While pondering our talk a few hours later, he had a phone conversation with his son where he caught himself telling the boy, "It's because I care I keep saying this over and over." His son replied, "That's the problem, you care too much, Dad." He saw how he was pushing the boy away and stopping rapport or deeper communication because of his overcare. People try to chase relationship rapport through overcare, then can't understand how they are repelling deeper resonance. Many parents will say, "But if I'm not worrying, I'm not caring." As you look deeper, you can see that worry is the wanton exaggeration of care and produces non-effective results. It is a total deficit in energy expenditure. When worry drains you, FREEZE-FRAME, take yourself back to the heart and find the original feeling of care, why you cared in the first place. This shifts you to a heart perception where you can drop the worry and enhance your power to act creatively.

The Real Drug Problem

One of the major concerns of parents today is about children taking drugs. It's a parenting issue that deserves much care, but here's how overcare can harm family members as much as taking drugs. Society fears drugs because they generate hormonal releases and biochemical imbalances which can scramble the mind and devastate the body. Yet, overcare attitudes cause similar devastation to people's internal drugstore. Continuous overcare is itself a potent drug in its effect on the hormonal and immune systems. Many ailments that contribute to the drug crisis and the health care crisis today are caused by overcare. Overcare is insidious because people don't know they're doing it or don't realize the consequences. As the immune and hormonal systems remain imbalanced by overcare in the form of insecurity, fear, or anxiety, people feel propelled to overeat or not eat, go on alcohol binges, take drugs, etc. Street drugs and prescription drugs are more obvious than overcare, but overcare acts as a continuous drug which depletes the system, accelerates the aging process, and is self-prescribed through repetitive thoughts and attitudes. As you realize that it's *overcare* that makes life worse for yourself and your children, you will understand that it's worth a little practice to balance your care.

On issues like children abusing drugs or alcohol, parents could easily feel, *"How could I not overcare about that!"* Through awareness, you can realize that *balanced care* is more powerful and effective, producing potent regenerative hormones within your system along with intuitive awareness that results in intelligent action. Finally, it's through *intelligence* that society's drug and health problems can be resolved.

Mass consciousness has unconsciously embraced overcare due to "hand-me-down" attitudes, a reverberation of pervading social concepts that encourage emotional over-identity. Of course, it's not just emotional over-identity with children's issues. Emotional over-identity about friends, relatives, pets, work, sports, vanity, health, social causes, etc., all create overcare. As I write this book, millions of people are emotionally over-identified with the O.J. Simpson trial, with job security, or with the world's ecological problems, to name a few current issues. What most don't realize is that overcare is draining the possibilities for creative outcomes relative to any of these issues. Overcare drains the emotional nature of the individual, the family, and the social community.

As emotional stamina is drained by overcare, it creates a lackluster quality in day-to-day experiences. When emotional quality is low, we mechanically operate at half-mast; our peace, fun and power to adapt are significantly reduced. If the drain continues, it results in low-grade depression which can then turn into hopelessness and despair. To prevent this downward spiral, identify your areas of overcare, then from your heart practice Freeze-Framing each issue and going back to an attitude of balanced care. This stops the drain on your emotional energy reservoir. Most people don't realize how much free energy they would accumulate by stopping payment on emotional drains. Freeze-Framing helps you self-police this process and bring your care back into balance. This results in increased energy, quality, and *adaptability*.

Adaptability

Adaptability is an essential quality unto itself, requiring mental and emotional management and stamina. *The more power you have to adapt to change, the more power you have to create changes that can improve your life.* Often people complain they don't have any power to change things, not realizing they've drained their power through not being able to adapt to what's already done. People lose tremendous amounts of energy reacting to what they read in the newspaper or see on TV, or reacting to events in the past, forgetting that *their reaction has no impact on that event.* They think overcare motivates productive action. It doesn't. Overcare incapacitates, squelches clarity, creates fear, and dilutes creative capacity. For example, when a child disappoints you, or fails a major test at school, or is caught taking drugs, if you don't stop overcare and learn to adapt, you drain your creative capacity to help him make productive changes. Adapting is not condoning a child's misbehavior. It's understanding that what's done is done, then moving forward so you can take appropriate action.

Understanding the purpose of adaptability and the type of energy it takes to manifest it, is extremely important in this era of rapid change. It's critical that people learn to manage their mental and emotional energies so they can adapt to the unpredictable, whether in parenting, relationships, work, or in social or natural disasters. *You eventually have to adapt anyhow.* Overcare lengthens the adaptation time and blocks hope for new solutions. Adapting through balanced care saves energy and shortens the time it takes to find new possibilities.

You can see how quickly children often adapt to change. Many parents have seen a child set on wanting something he can't have, but after one sincere talk the child lets it go. The parent is surprised because she knew that just a few minutes earlier the child was extremely stressed-out and bent on what he wanted. That's a testimony to the power of adaptability that the young have naturally until they diminish it through society's hand-me-down concepts and overcare. As adults practice flexibility, pliability, and resilience to release their overcares, they will recoup that childlike spirit.

Let's look at how some of the parents who identified their overcares during the Empowered Parent seminar resolved them.

Example: Overexplaining everything, wanting to make sure my child "gets it," wanting him to understand so I nag or lecture, yet I still can't "get through" to him.

After this parent Freeze-Framed, using a FREEZE-FRAME worksheet to help him gain clarity, he realized his head reaction was worry and anxiety that he wasn't a good enough parent. Feeling insecure, he would nag more, trying harder and harder. Freeze-Framing back to balanced care, his heart intuition response was that his first step would be to listen to his son more deeply from the heart and to practice more listening than talking until the deeper care connection was re-established between them. As he discussed this insight with the other parents, they realized how overcare numbs people from feeling connected with the original care they once felt in a relationship. Once overcare sets in, it gets harder to re-experience the quality moments that people have shared with each other in the past. That's why parents often say, "I don't know what happened, for years my child and I were so close, and now we're not even on the same wavelength when we try to communicate."

Overcare literally creates a different wavelength that repels deeper connection. It's like listening to a radio station with the dial stuck between the station and static. When this happens between parents and children, it creates the popular term "communication gap." It's *overcare* that creates the static and gaps; it's *balanced care* that hones in on the station for enriched communication.

The Power of Sincere Care

When people are asked to remember a person who meant a lot to them in life — a teacher, a friend, a parent, a grandparent — they usually remember a person who really cared and understood them. Think back in your own life. Was there someone who stands out in your memory because they really cared about you?

When I was a boy, I was a discipline problem and did not do well in school. The only time my grades even began to pick up was with one teacher who genuinely wanted to help me. Other teachers had tried, but there was something different about Ms. Nelson. She didn't nag me, but had a genuine interest in my well-being and complimented me on what I did do well. I really liked Ms. Nelson, so I wanted to do better. She sincerely cared! The experience of sincere care is inspiring. Sincere care is the missing ingredient for a more harmonious and productive work, home, or community environment. Sincere care is the cohesive substance that preserves relationships. It helps waive the dislikes and annoyances parents have with children by providing balanced understanding. The world is starving for real care. Balanced care nurtures and heals, spawning security and support for all involved.

If people mathematically understood the energy lost or saved in relation to care, learning the difference between *balanced care* and *overcare* would be a required course in standard educational curricula. This one course would solve a large number of problems in children, problems between family members, problems within school systems, as well as facilitate a child's overall learning capacities. Most learning abilities are enhanced when the static of overcare about *so many things* is removed from the inner mental state. If children are taught to understand the difference between *care* and *overcare* at an early age, this will act as preventive maintenance to minimize communication problems as they grow up and become parents of the next generation.

To remove overcare takes practice. To identify and acknowledge it is the first and most important step. FREEZE-FRAME can take the worry out of your care. It pinpoints where your care is stress-producing and has turned to overcare. Following the steps of FREEZE-FRAME will show you how to consciously shift your perception back to balanced care which stops payment on energy leaks and static accumulation. As you become practiced, remembering the energy you save helps give you more power to "just say no," go to your heart when overcare starts, and find a perception shift. Once you make a perception shift from the heart, then the head will follow suit and provide a new, more effective perspective.

Vicky's seventeen year old daughter Ginny did not come home from a date until 3:00 a.m. She had agreed to be home by her midnight curfew. The last time this happened Vicky was frantic with worry and cried for hours while she waited for the sound of the door opening. This time when the worry started and she could feel her tears rise, she practiced Freeze-Framing. Vicky had recently attended a HeartMath *Inner Quality Management*® training at her company where she learned about overcare. She Freeze-Framed and was able to "just say no" to the worry and the tears. She listened deeply to her heart's common sense and her intuition told her that Ginny was probably just fine. Whatever her daughter was doing, worrying and crying would not help. Vicky's perception shifted to a heart understanding that although the family had agreed to a midnight curfew, her daughter did not believe in it and had no intention of abiding by it. Vicky realized she needed to have an honest talk with her daughter.

Much internal stress is generated by an ongoing inner argument between people's head and heart perceptions. Even when we are not consciously aware of it, there's often an inner frequency war with two sides competing for the spotlight. It's not that the head and heart are really staged against each other like good and bad guys; it's that they are randomly trying to find coherent interaction. The challenge is that head/heart coherence has to be instigated through conscious effort. That potential is within each person. It's easier than people might think to create the balanced adventure between head and heart, once they are aware of the enormous benefits. This is what the IHM research laboratory is showing — that attitudes which are based on heart and head teamwork enrich communication and nourish the entire human system, right down to the immune and hormonal systems. *Balanced care* is an example of beneficial teamwork, while attitudes of *overcare* generate cross-frequencies between heart and head that have continuous detrimental effects.

Often people know deep in the heart that what they call care is draining them and even get mad that the care they are putting out is draining. They say, "By god I'm tired of it. Just let him go, I'm tired of caring." So parents let their kids go, not from weaning them away, but from burn-out. The result is no care. People don't realize that overcare begets more overcare until you are so drained you don't care anymore.

What happens when someone abruptly stops caring? I had a friend who was my main buddy after school. As teenagers, we talked about girls, school, cars, everything, and covered for each other when one of us got into trouble. One day he ditched me and started hanging out with another group of guys. He didn't say why, and I was too "cool" to ask. But inside I felt hurt, betrayed, lost, like a ship at sea. It's grim when a feeling of closeness ends. I overcared about this hurt until I didn't care anymore I was so drained. If I had known how to use my heart intelligence at that age, I would have realized I needed to talk to him in order to free myself.

Overcare can seem so natural or justified and that's the problem with it. But anxiety, despair, and depression aren't really natural, just common. Hand-me-down themes of society need addressing if parents are going to have basic peace and not hand over their power, fun, and quality of life to draining overcare.

Single Parenting

Overcare is a major issue for single parents; understanding it is a major bailout. Angelina is a single, working mother of two teenage boys. When she attended IHM's Empowered Parent seminar, she had been divorced for six years and felt guilty about her sons not having a male role model in the home. She said learning the difference between care and overcare turned on a light bulb inside her. At the seminar, she listed her overcares on a FREEZE-FRAME assets/deficits sheet.

On the <u>deficits</u> side she wrote:

- Feeling guilty about being a single parent and not having the perfect family model.

- Boys don't have male role model.

- Isolation from other adults as a single parent, and overcaring that I can't give my children what they need.

- Hung up on what other parents think, what my child's teacher thinks, or how society looks at me as a single parent.

- Overcaring about whether my kids like me. Wanting their approval. Wanting them to like me all the time.

On the <u>assets</u> side she wrote:

- At peace being single, I enjoy my kids more, too many arguments when I was with my husband, it was destructive to the boys.

- Better no father in the house if he's not going to be a real "role model."

- My boys are okay. They are having fun, doing fine in school. I have friends. My overcare about what people might think has prevented me from sharing my real self with them.

- I am giving my sons the best I can.

In Freeze-Framing her conclusion, Angelina had a heart perception of the many hours she'd spent over the past six years worrying about the deficits and forgetting the assets. It's not that she hadn't thought about the assets before. It's that she never had the clarity that her heart feelings were now providing. Freeze-Framing resolved the internal confusion between her head and heart and enabled her to take a deeper look at what was real. By releasing overcare, she gained intuitive clarity that she had made the right decision to divorce her husband and that the deficits weren't even real. She saw that it was overcare that was making them seem real, occupying her thoughts, draining her energy and isolating her. Angelina's heart intelligence showed her how buying into hand-me-down concepts about single parenting had imprisoned her. She felt released and empowered with new tools to move forward and stop bleeding her energy in useless guilt or worry about what others might think. She later said, *"Understanding balanced care gave me back my life."*

Many parents suffer overcares similar to Angelina's and need to make a realistic assessment of their situation. Overcare endlessly churns problems, worries, and hand-me-down programs in the mind, blocking heart intelligence. As of 1995, 12.9 million children in the USA live in single-parent homes. Balanced care is dealing with what is. What's done is done. Dealing with what is leads to new effectiveness and quality. It's not whether a child is brought up in a single family, foster family, or traditional family that matters most. It's the quality of love and care, or the lack of it, that matters.

Hand-me-down Ideas

Hand-me-down ideas set up a comparative structure where you're the victim and can't win. Buying into a hand-me-down formula can cause the very problem you are overcaring about. Here's a graphic example of how overcare can at times cause or perpetuate what you don't want. When I was nine I went to live with my grandparents. My grandmother was always overcaring about something. She would feed all the dogs from the neighborhood daily because she hated to throw food away. Then she would literally cry because the dogs kept the yard torn up. My grandfather kept telling her, "Don't feed the dogs and you won't have to keep picking up the trash." But she couldn't stop. She didn't have much money and wouldn't waste a scrap. Like many kids, I was told to clean my plate whether I was hungry or not because starving kids in foreign countries didn't have any food. I was thirty pounds overweight before I realized that the left-over food on my plate wasn't going to reach the starving kids in India anyway, though I had compassion for their situation. I dropped the hand-me-down concept about food and found balance in my eating. The main reason that people like my grandmother don't realize that overcare saps energy is because it's hidden behind good intentions of care. I've seen parents cry because their kids abused money or privileges, yet they kept on giving to them in excess because of overcare. The parents' intentions were good. They were trying to be responsive to duty and be accepted by their children.

Women and Overcare

Women find themselves in more obvious overcare predicaments and seem more vulnerable to overcare than men, but here's why. They have the dominant role in parenting due to inborn, natural sensitivities to care for a child. As more women have joined the workforce, their natural nurturing care and sensitivity has been a positive add-on. But when nurturing turns to overcare, it blocks clarity and emotionally drains. That's why men often accuse women of being unable to make the tough decisions. In general, women also have more thresholds of overcare to address due to a male-dominant society, so it's easier for them to feel victimized by unfair social structures. This fosters a consistent low-grade overcare in numerous women. When women make a sincere effort to identify overcare, then bring it back to balanced care, they can overcome unfairness *internally*. They gain greater ability to access the intuitive intelligence from the heart that is needed to *change things* rather than feel like pawns in hand-me-down structures.

It may seem I'm straying from the theme of parenting, but a lot of women don't have much energy left for parenting because of being drained by all these issues. For example, a major issue among women is the tug of war between work, family, and personal time. How could that not result in an energy deficit from overcare? This tug-of-war isn't going to change overnight, and the fairy godmother of fairness isn't going to appear and make it all okay. But you *can* make it better. How? By using the tools in this book, you *build your own hope*. Hope is free energy for initiatives of change. Despair becomes a negative entrainment pattern that feeds itself in the absence of hope. That's why learning to generate your own hope from heart intelligence can help free you from a possible one-way trip to exhaustion. Developing heart perception provides an intuitive exit off the treadmill, and is a vehicle for creating your own peace. As you make sincere efforts to use the tools HEART LOCK-IN and FREEZE-FRAME, they increase your internal awareness regarding situations. This results in leveraged intelligence to make effective changes. Sincerely identify overcares, then use heart perception to re-balance your care. Productive action and increased peace will follow naturally.

A Stand versus A Stance

Many women who have applied the HeartMath system have a new excitement in realizing the power of a *heart stand* versus a *mind stance* when dealing with these monumental issues at hand. A *heart stand* fortifies the bail-out process, while a *mind stance* often leads to debilitation and less accomplished than hoped for, in spite of all the effort invested. That's not to say progress hasn't been made in women's issues, but to yield a higher ratio of results, what's required is leveraged intelligence through intuitive perception from the heart. This can be the hope for completion of long deserved efforts.

Increasing numbers of fathers also find themselves in a single parent role, or sharing more childcare and household responsibilities with busy working wives. As men assume a more traditionally female role in nurturing children, cooking, and cleaning, new sensitivities are demanded. They start to experience the same types of overcares that women have to address. Fathers experience increasing conflict between work, family, and personal time. Men comment on their overworked and exhausted generation, but feel they are working hard for their future and for their children. They see their children, the next generation, as the hope for the future. Unless children learn something new to prevent the same overcare hand-me-downs that are draining their parents, they will end up saying the same thing — that their children, the next generation, are the hope for the future and so the story goes on until something changes. *Heartfelt intuition is the balancing factor for both men and women.* When men and women alike understand that increasing intuition is the new momentum for making effective decisions, they will address the overcare issues within themselves that reduce emotional stamina. Reduced stamina leads to depletion and a "hamster wheel" existence. Freeze-Framing overcare conserves energy and creates a time shift by stopping time waste from mental and emotional worry, anxiety, or guilt. You create time and energy to do what's important to you.

Emotional Upsets and Heartaches

When children have emotional upsets or heartaches, parents often find it difficult not to overcare. Emotional upsets require intuitive listening to understand what's behind them and provide balanced care and guidance. If your son is distressed because he didn't make the Little League line-up, ask him how that makes him feel, then patiently wait. *Just listen.* After you hear him out, help him find alternative attitudes and solutions. If he wants to be on the team next year, could he practice now? If he says yes, talk with the coach about a practice program. If he says no, explore other sports or hobbies he may enjoy.

Children develop best in surroundings in which they have occasions to bruise their knees and break their hearts in childlike fashion. Minor hurts and scrapes assist them in saving their necks or suffering heartaches later in life. Overcaring parents rob children of that experience and instruction. For example, whenever three year old Michael stumbled and fell, or was teased by another child, or couldn't have an object he wanted, he would let out a blood-curdling shriek, and cry inconsolably until his mother comforted him. Mother and son engaged in an ongoing ritual that went like this: "You poor thing, let Mommy fix it and make it all better." As Mommy pampered him with kisses, hugs, a glass of juice, a cracker, promises to find him another toy, etc., Michael's whimpers would lessen. He would only stop after having extracted a full dose of sympathy and promises from his mother.

Allowing children to escape consequences is not love. If Michael's mother continues her over-protective approach, when he's older he'll expect life to pamper him as his mother did. Children require love and balanced care, not over-coddling, to help them bear the discomfort, upset, or heartache it takes to master the challenging waves of life. When a child has a physical discomfort, balanced care would be to stay calm as you tend to the situation. For example, a five year old scrapes her elbow and it's bleeding. At the sight of blood she sobs. You can't tell if she's really hurting or scared. Calmly say, "Let's go find a band-aid," and quietly lead her to the medicine cabinet. Staying balanced reassures her there's no need to panic. Then you can objectively assess the injury and take appropriate action. Children are always bruising knees, scraping arms, and bumping heads. They fall off bikes, trip over toys, and stub their toes. If you are loving and heart coherent with a child, you can often release a minor hurt with humor. When a four year old falls off his scooter and starts to cry, from the heart you can say, "Oh no, is the sidewalk hurt?" You direct the attention to the child caring about the sidewalk, so he naturally is in the heart caring about the sidewalk. Then the mother and child can care, giggle, and laugh together. Sometimes when children are hurt they need a softer, gentler energy. But if you say, "Oh my gosh, the poor baby's hurt," the child will get into a head frequency of "poor me." *Overcare encourages self-pity.* As a parent, approach discomforts with balanced care. Then your child will learn to do the same.

Heartaches are deeper emotional traumas. Heartache is caused by broken mental expectations or attachments, backed with emotional investment. The mind will not stop churning over the hurt. To illustrate: Your eight year old daughter's closest friends are invited to a birthday party, but she is not. She doesn't understand why and feels heartbroken. What does a parent do? It's helpful to let her talk, as it may reveal clues. As with any emotional upset, draw out her feelings, but stay emotionally balanced yourself. Don't respond with righteous indignation: "What's wrong with that girl's mother! Doesn't she know you are one of her daughter's friends?" Neither encourage self-pity: "Oh you poor darling, I feel so sorry for you." As children learn that life has its disappointments and neither blaming others nor self-pity helps, they'll look for alternate solutions. If the heartache continues, call the birthday child's mother and sincerely explain the problem. Find out the facts from a neutral position. Perhaps the mother only has space for a few children. Maybe she doesn't realize how close your daughter feels to her child. Or maybe the girls had a quarrel. As a parent, the more you can find out why to help explain the real reason, the easier it will be for your child to release the pain.

Heartaches occur when we perceive that we have lost something that we cared about deeply. Heartaches range from crises such as, "Why did my parents divorce?" "Why did my daddy die?" "Why did my girlfriend reject me?" to issues like, "Why won't the other boys play with me?" When the heart aches, people always ask, "Why?" If it's the head asking why, it prolongs the aching heart, as the head tries to find answers by replaying the anger and hurt over and over. If it's the heart asking why, sincerely wanting to understand, even in tragic situations the intuition will eventually play out answers and solutions. That's what heart intelligence is all about.

When parents get emotionally upset, children also tend to overcare and worry until they learn balanced care from an adult role model. If you are emotionally upset because of something your child has done, don't place the blame for your hurt or anger on the child. For example, if you're upset because your child was late for dinner and didn't call, don't burst forth with, "I've told you a million times to call if you're going to be late. You make me so angry!" Tell your son how you feel about his actions but take responsibility for your own feelings. FREEZE-FRAME and ask your heart intelligence to guide you. You might say, "We agreed you would be home by dinnertime. I didn't know where you were and I was very angry that you didn't call." Parents need to realize the purpose of expressing feelings is to feature the problem and take responsibility for one's own reaction. It's okay for children to see a parent's moments of emotion, but don't make them accountable. *You are responsible for your feelings, not your child.* As parents, if we humiliate or blame children for our anger, our most effective action is to apologize. If you scream at your child or slap him out of anger, say "I'm sorry" and explain from the heart why you were so upset. Tell him, "You broke a rule and therefore you will be grounded for two days. I'm sorry I hit you. I had a rough day at the office, then when you didn't call to say you'd be late I got mad." Don't beg forgiveness out of a need to be liked or to have your child's approval. Simply speak your truth through the heart and apologize. Usually parents don't do that. If parents have continuous stress, it's hard for a child not to take on the parents' stress as well. When you sincerely apologize, it releases your stress and your child's stress. That's loving yourself and your child and improves communication. Actually, children are very forgiving. They're sincerely forgiving.

Practicing True Care — For Yourself and Your Child

The core element of good parenting is to practice consistency and understanding. *The first step is knowing you love your child, wanting the most for him or her.* This allows you to align your motives with your core values, putting you in touch with your real heart. Love is powerful. When you feel love and want the best for someone, you come into resonance and coherence with that person's heart. Being heart coherent with a child helps prevent and remedy communication gaps. The HEART LOCK-IN tool helps you find that feeling of love and heart coherence.

The second step is to use the tool FREEZE-FRAME. This tool helps you release any judgments, frustration, anxiety, negative attitudes, or reactiveness toward your child. Observe what is happening in each problematic scene with your child. Learn how to ask your heart intelligence, "Why does he or she behave in this manner?" Ask yourself,

"What am I, as the parent, doing about the situation?" As you FREEZE-FRAME, ask your heart intelligence to help you understand your child's feelings. Sincerely listen to your heart intuitive answers. Write them down and see if they help. Follow your heart intelligence.

FREEZE-FRAME your overcares and find balanced care. Bringing overcare back to true care creates changes in how you feel, giving you new perspectives for making more loving and intelligent choices. You will comprehend true care as a powerful energy, one that revitalizes and activates the hormonal system, providing a sense of fulfillment and heart-warming textures to life. As you practice these tools and teach them to your children, you will understand both your child and yourself in new ways. When times are tough, people naturally try to go to their hearts to unearth deeper feelings (and intelligence) for security and strength. The heart is the inner storehouse of common-sense wisdom and love. Under our society's hand-me-down stress conditioning, it's hard to find those clear intuitive answers unless you know how to release overcare — and have tools to help you.

Parents have a lot on their shoulders today — life is just faster. The parent's childlike spirit, as well as the child's spirit, can be covered up and repressed by overcare and anxiety conditioning. Anxiety can become so ingrained and so continually reinforced and amplified by society, that the spirit can get totally lost. I have compassion for all concerned, but it doesn't have to be this way. You and your family do have a choice to see the world from a more balanced and hopeful perspective, and find workable solutions for any overcare or stress gridlock. When you delight in parenting, whether it's teaching a child to ride her first bike or having a sincere heart-to-heart talk about a problem, then parenting is truly rewarding. Finding solutions to challenges warms the heart. As the heart is warmed, life has meaning.

Chapter 7

Effective Communication

Society's values are undergoing a paradigm shift. As I've said, a paradigm is a foundation from which to perceive the world. Based on our foundational perceptions, we construct decisions and responses to the world around us. "Who am I?" "Where am I going?" "What do I believe?" become primary questions in self-reflection and discussion in the aftereffects and aftermaths of this shift.

One teen viewing from a head perspective answered these questions in the following way:

"Who am I?"
    "I'm Mark. I'm 14 years old and I'm a tennis player."

"Where am I going?"
    "I'm going to finish high school, maybe go to college, then get a job and make some money."

"What do I believe?"
    "I believe in gun control. There's too much crime."

From the heart perspective, a teen would answer from another level. Here's how Christian, a thirteen year old who practices the HeartMath tools responded:

"Who am I?"

"I'm just another person. I am my own self. I'm pretty lucky 'cause I've got a pretty easy life compared to a lot of people."

"Where am I going?"

"Up! I see life like a tree. I'm the big black ant climbing up the tree. You get to a branch and life is a choice. You can go up the trunk of the tree or off on a branch. There are lots of branches. The heart of a tree is in the trunk, the good old juicy part of the tree. Some people go off on a branch and get in trouble. The branch will start to break and you get caught. Then you have the choice if you want to tell the truth and get back to the heart of the tree. But you can lie and fall, and have a long walk back up the tree to where you were. You have to be on your toes."

"What do I believe?"

"I believe that life's kind of like a Nintendo® game. You learn how to play the game at each level. Everyone's their own individual person. One person might think totally different from another. I see everyone with their own little ideas. But everyone's just the same basically."

It's the combination of both heart and head that brings the greater intelligence and real understanding needed to reconstruct our society. As I've said, children are not taught how to manage the head or how to develop the heart. They are taught to use the head in school, to direct it in analytical thought, but not to calm it down or balance it with heart intelligence. As a result, they perceive life and communicate from insecure head perceptions, as does society around them. When the head functions in a joint venture with the heart, children develop wisdom, power, and integrity in making choices and in their communication.

Communicating Discipline to Children

Discipline is essential for developing wisdom and integrity. Discipline is love in action. Therefore, if you really do love a child, you care enough to discipline him. You're getting him ready for life, and life has its natural laws and man-made laws, called bottom-lines. This chapter will support discipline from a constructive, stable, adult perspective. Children prosper from bottom-lines and routines. In effect, this builds a good foundation. The word discipline originates from "disciple," an adherent of a teacher. In Webster's New World Dictionary, discipline includes: "training that develops self-control, orderliness and efficiency; acceptance of or submission to authority and control; a system of rules." In summary, discipline is an action taken to educate oneself or another in order to function in this world. Parents need to encourage children to follow rules because they understand them, not because they fear counter-blows. From the heart, children can always understand a reasonable rule or bottom-line, even though they may not always like it. The true goal of discipline is *self-discipline.*

One of the keys to productive discipline is for the parent to maintain mental and emotional consistency while training the child. Heart intelligence provides clear decisions and actions concerning rules, a routine bottom-line and consequences. Discuss these with your child in calm communication. Most discipline becomes effective and beneficial when the parent quietly and rationally communicates.

Sit down with your child and have a strategic discussion. Lay out your bottom-line boundaries and the reasons why. Then ask your child if he understands. Have him repeat back to you each bottom-line rule and why it's needed. Ask him what he thinks. Listen from the heart deeply to your child's response. If he does not agree with a rule or doesn't understand it, patiently explain in more depth why the rule is needed. Explain why it's for his own good or for his protection. For example, if you are telling a child he must be in bed by 8:00 p.m. every night, explain that he needs more sleep to help him be less moody, concentrate better in school, or whatever your reason may be.

As the heart expands, a clearer definition of rules and consequences will manifest. Communicate these updates to the child. Parents repeatedly assume children comprehend the family statutes. This is not always true. Children do not know what a parent wants if the communication involves screaming or the rule is not clearly explained or understood. Once you are certain your child clearly understands, then from a business-like heart remind her if she forgets. If you remind her too often, it turns into nagging. To avoid nagging, allow for common-sense time intervals between reminders, maybe once a week. When she does forget, you still need to enforce your bottom-line consequences. Your heart intuition can guide you in making remembering a fun game instead of a drag.

Many parents try to discipline on the run. With a fast-paced life, parents often find themselves juggling two or three activities at once on a tight time schedule. Whether it's racing at warp speed to get everyone off to work and school each morning, or chauffeuring children to dental appointments, piano lessons, Girl Scouts, etc., many parents feel continually rushed. One mother, Sharon, said her greatest stress and aggravation was with . . . how . . . slowly . . . her . . . kids . . . moved. She was constantly hurrying them and yelling at them to put on coats, lock doors, and get in the car so they wouldn't be late. Rushing, yelling, nagging and threatening discipline had become her way of life. She finally realized this approach was totally ineffective and draining.

Parental Assessment

Assessing children accurately and responding effectively requires having the qualification to communicate, interpret, and understand their changing feelings and moods — like frustration, anger, excitement, or love. Each child has different characteristics and will go through various mood fluctuations. If you have three children of different ages, one could be moody, another exuberant, and the third very willful. As a parent, you continually receive new data and compare it with what you already know. The challenge then is how to respond to all the data. Are your current assessments coming from head reactions, from opinions and concepts, or from your true heart intelligence? Recognize a quality or character trait in your child but if you disagree with it, don't judge; just love the child to receive intuitional understanding. Try to see from your child's eyes. FREEZE-FRAME, send love and ask yourself, "What is my child perceiving?" Then listen to your heart. Love offers children the latitude to be themselves. Children and life are always changing and judgments limit a parent's perception, blocking the next level of knowingness.

Children who are hyperactive can be especially trying. To find balanced care requires a lot of compassion and love for yourself. A hyperactive child I've worked with has a need to explore and touch everything that attracts his attention. Because he moves so fast from one thing to the next, if he touches something fragile it's likely to break. You can tell him, "Don't touch," a hundred times and it's as if he has never heard you. It's simple for a parent to feel he's ignoring you on purpose.

Hyperactive children are often labeled as having Attention Deficit Disorder (ADD). This is a huge issue in schools today as more children are being labeled ADD. Who wouldn't be challenged by children who have difficulty sitting still or focusing on one thing for any length of time, who constantly disrupt classroom and family activities and are often loud? Increasingly, children labeled ADD are medicated with drugs that have strong side effects. It's important to realize that a hyperactive child is easily overstimulated. In today's overstimulated society, it is essential that parents and teachers find ways to help children find balance. While not a cure-all, the HeartMath tools have helped many hyperactive children better manage themselves, and helped many parents better understand the inner world of their hyperactive children.

Very inward, shy children are actually hyperactive on the inside. They, too, are sensitive to overstimulation, but their reaction is to withdraw and cut off external stimuli. If a parent doesn't understand this oversensitivity, an introverted child can be difficult. The shy child may not explore or express much outwardly. Disappointed parents who try so hard to please don't see this simply as a personality trait. They perceive that their introverted child is intentionally baffling and balking. The messages the child dispenses are ambiguous; there seems to be no reason for the child's inward behavior. So the parents look for motives in an effort to understand what is going on. They feel the child is deliberately cutting off from them and giving them trouble. This causes a parent to feel victimized, exhausted, and incompetent.

The key to assessing and intuitively understanding children's unique personality traits and needs is to listen to their hearts. Parents, please want to listen to your child's heart. It's the heart you're trying to listen to, not all the facts. When you know what's in your child's heart — the real underlying feelings — then you sincerely can find effective solutions. You will understand your child's perceptions and be able to explain yourself clearly. Discipline becomes a natural, coherent flow within the household. Communicating your bottom-line rules, making sure your children understand them, and enforcing them consistently without yelling, nagging, or threatening, is essential for effective discipline. When consequences are clear and discipline is not based on threats or fear, children do understand. While it's easy to feel there's no time for calm communication and follow through, you will actually save loads of time, energy, and stress in the long run.

An Important Tool for Parenting — Sincere Communication and Deep Listening

Children need to feel that their parents sincerely want to understand them. When parents are consciously wanting to understand a child, the heart energy is amplified. Sincerity opens the heart and it opens up communication. Sincere communication involves first listening deeply from your own heart, then sincerely speaking your truth from the heart. An important part of deep listening is what I call a *hearing ability* — the ability to hear others at the essence level beneath their words. Most of us have been in conversations where we felt we weren't being heard. Or maybe the words were heard, but our feelings and our real meaning were not heard. A deep hearing ability ensures that you are listening to your child with care and respect. When negative emotions are raining, be a sincere listener exclusively. Try not to probe for just the facts. When fierce feelings occur, send your child love to calm the storm. If you smash your child with judgment, you will quash communication. Children swiftly unmask how vulnerable they truly are as they venture to be themselves. As you listen deeply from the heart, a child feels your love and this helps open the intuitional field. The intuitive connection reduces miscommunications between parent and child.

The Intuitive Listening Tool

To develop INTUITIVE LISTENING, there are three essential elements to be aware of while you listen to another person speak:

1. **Word Level** — what is actually said.

2. **Feeling Level** — the feeling or frequencies behind the words.

3. **Essence Level** — the real meaning.

The Steps of INTUITIVE LISTENING:

Step 1 — Deeply listen to your own heart. Ask your heart intelligence to help you. FREEZE-FRAME your head thoughts and let them go, while you quietly tune into your own heart.

Step 2 — Deeply listen to other people's hearts when they talk to you. Do the same as in Step 1 while listening to someone else. When the other person first starts to talk, FREEZE-FRAME to shift your focus away from the mind and emotions and into your heart. By listening to people's hearts speak, you get the wider picture — their frequency, or feelings, and the deeper meaning behind their words.

Step 3 — Hear them out; don't interrupt (interrupting is a head reaction). Stay in your heart as they speak. If your mind comes up with answers or arguments as they are talking, make efforts to bring those thoughts back to the heart and wait until they are done speaking. If your thoughts are important, you won't forget. It's more important to hear people out than to interrupt with your response. It saves energy.

Step 4 — Pause 10-20 seconds before responding. Tell them you need a moment before you respond. Use that time to listen deeply to your own heart for intuitive direction. Access your heart and then speak your truth.

Step 5 — Speak your truth from a clear "business" heart. Heart intuition is not overly emotional. It gets down to business, but with sincerity and care. Truth from the heart has both clarity and compassion.

How to Apply Intuitive Listening

From this five-step framework, here's how to apply INTUITIVE LIS-TENING with your child. Define what you intend to tell your child ahead of time. As I mentioned earlier, the first step is to love your child; the second is to FREEZE-FRAME to access a deeper intuitive perspective, release overcare and find balanced care. Lay out the communication from a loving heart in a business-like way. Say something similar to the following, tailored to your situation. Cindy is four years old and hates to bathe. It's always a fight to get her into the tub. After practicing the above steps, her mother said: *"I have been thinking about you fighting me every time you need to take a bath. The new rule is that this is not allowed. I'm glad you like to play outside. People bathe after they play. Please try not to argue when I say it's time for a bath. If you can't control yourself, you'll have to go to bed without your bedtime story."*

Eight year old Jason refused to do his chores, which were making his bed each day, putting his dirty clothes in the hamper, and sweeping the kitchen floor after supper. His parents had bribed him with promises of new toys but that didn't work. He'd do his chores for two days, forget, then refuse to do them at all. His father practiced the HeartMath steps, then laid out the new rule. *"I have been thinking about your chores. I notice you forget to do them, then mom and I nag you about them and you still refuse to do them. We don't want to nag anymore. The new rule is this: We will post your chores on the back of your bedroom door to help you remember. If you do not do your chores each day, you will not be allowed to play video games for the next three days."*

Make sure your child has heard and understood you. Encourage him to do his best. As a child realizes levels of success, it is important to acknowledge the efforts made. Of course, you don't need to rant with extreme emotional excitement about every little task well done. If Jason's father applauds him each time he sweeps the kitchen floor, Jason will feel belittled. Overdone praise and attention confuses a child. Respect that you expect him to behave. At the same time, sincere appreciation lets a child know that you've perceived his efforts. Be a whole-hearted parent.

Perceptions, Actions, and Consequences

As I've said, increased parental stress is due largely to misunderstanding children's perceptions and feelings. Self-empowerment is the skill to select, from the heart's perception, an appropriate response to a feeling. First acknowledge that perceptions and feelings do not in themselves cause actions. Actions result from choices the mind formulates on how to respond to a perception or a feeling. If taken to the heart, the heart intuition will provide a new perception and a new feeling. This will result in a different action than if the perception or feeling is taken only to the head. The mind formulates choices based on the data it sees. This happens at very high speed. That's why FREEZE-FRAME and INTUITIVE LISTENING are so important. These tools slow down the process so people can understand it and make efficient heart intelligent choices. Keith's story on page 46 is a good example of how children practicing FREEZE-FRAME can observe their internal process and understand the relationship between their perceptions and their actions. Children and adults enhance self-empowerment as they understand the coherence between perceptions and actions, and the coherence between actions and consequences.

Let me illustrate by slow-framing a family argument. Ten year old Craig kicked his seven year old sister Cathy. She yelled, "Don't do that!" and hit him back. The father shouted, "Stop it, both of you." "He kicked me first," Cathy protested. Dad screamed, "I don't care. Shut up! We don't get angry in this house! Go to your room if you can't control yourself!" This entire interaction occurred at high speed in less than thirty seconds. Parents who scream at their children teach them to avoid communication of their perceptions. Instead, if parents observe with balanced care what children are experiencing they can orchestrate a more constructive outcome. Extend guidance to children on how to decipher their perceptions. This permits children to express perceptions and feelings as their own experience. Then provide feedback while establishing limits on how feelings may be aired.

Now let's replay the above example. Instead of denying everyone's feelings after Craig and Cathy fought, suppose Dad asked Craig why he kicked Cathy and what he was feeling. Craig muttered, "She was bothering me." It took a few questions to uncover his deeper reasons. Dad asked, "What was she doing?" The boy responded, "She was fidgeting." Cathy chimed in, "I was not. I wasn't doing anything!" Craig retorted, "You were too, you were moving all around." Dad intervened, "It's Craig's turn to talk, please let him finish." Addressing Craig, Dad asked, "Why did her fidgeting bother you?" "I couldn't concentrate on the book I was reading, so it made me angry," replied Craig. Dad answered, "Expressing how you feel by kicking is not allowed. If you kick again, you won't be allowed to watch TV for a week. Can you think of another way?" Craig offered that either he would ask Cathy to be quieter or he would move to the other side of the room to read. Dad asked Cathy why she was moving all around. Cathy replied that she didn't know. Upon further questioning, Cathy explained that she was bored with her coloring book and didn't know what to do with herself. Dad helped Cathy see how fidgeting could be distracting to Craig. They discussed what she could do the next time she feels restless. Dad also told Cathy that hitting back when someone kicks you isn't allowed either and she would have the same consequence as Craig. Seeing the relationship between perceptions, actions and consequences helps children *remember* to stop and assess their perceptions from the heart so they have the ability to choose a different action.

While this entire communication process may take a little time, it saves time and aggravation in the long run. Perceptions, feelings and actions happen so fast that children often get in trouble without knowing why or how to stop. A heart intelligent father's purpose here is for children to understand the formula: **I perceive, I act, I remember.** If I go with my head reaction, the consequence will be different than if I go to the heart and consider the situation first. For example, "I perceived my sister was distracting me, I felt anger, I kicked my sister, therefore I can't watch TV." So the next time Craig perceives his sister is distracting him and feels his anger rise, he can remember what happened last time and choose not to act. He can go to the heart to create another outcome and it becomes fun. For example, "I perceive my sister is distracting me, I start to yell, then I catch myself. I know where this is going to lead so let me FREEZE-FRAME quick and go to my heart. From my heart perception I now see my sister is bored. She's not bothering me on purpose so my anger goes away. I can ask her to please be quieter or I move to the other side of the room." Freeze-Framing develops remembering so it gets easier for children to see they have the power to choose. They know that they can use their FREEZE-FRAME tool when they need help fast. This is an example of what I mean by the "math" or psychological equations of heart intelligence — and why I call it HeartMath.

Children can become proficient in using their heart intelligence to select from a cluster of choices. As they practice these tools, children grow capable of rapidly recognizing the difference between head or heart perceptions, feelings, and actions. Thus, they gain self-empowerment. A key objective is to aid children in understanding that while feelings are real, they have a *choice* in how to deal with their feelings and their perceptions.

The Importance of Structure

Children need a "structure" to operate within, a conceptual framework of the family relationships and rules. Structure is the framing of a sequence of events to create everyday order. For example, a child who has no structure at meal times and is allowed to grab whatever he wants out of the fridge, quickly develops poor eating habits. Provide a framework that doesn't change with each emotional outburst. If the structure is that the child eat some vegetables at dinner before he gets dessert, but the parent caves in when the child screams and cries, the parent is breaking the structure. This causes confusion. Children need stable structures. Important structured events are meals, bedtime, playtime, and bathing. As a child grows, you can re-assess the structure to fit his expanding needs.

Are boundaries and bottom-lines necessary? In this parenting manual, they are an absolute. The raw fact that humans live in social clusters requires rules. The family is a grouping of bodies. A family's job is to prepare children for society, a larger grouping that most definitely has rules and regulations. Rules are needed for safety, less chaos, and to take care of the group whole. Classrooms that lack enforced rules aggravate teachers and children who really want to learn. The heart perception comprehends that without rules to maintain calm, children's energies become so amped that the teacher easily loses control. Learning becomes difficult. Families, classrooms, and businesses are more effective when they have rules designed to fulfill the needs of the whole. What would happen to a society without rules? It would be a mess. If there were no speed limits or stop signs, cars would crash into each other. If there were no laws enforced against people stealing or harming others, we'd be at the mercy of those who did not care. This is obvious.

Each family does not require the same amount or same type of rules. Rules are meant to help or protect children, but they are also meant to make a parent's life easier. Rules might be different for different family members, depending on their needs. Explain the reason for the differences to children. If one parent works a night shift, the rule may be you can't wake her up until noon but you can wake the other parent at 7:00 a.m. because he doesn't work at night. Stan overcared because his fourteen year old had more chores to do than his nine year old brother. The fourteen year old complained it was unfair, while the nine year old snickered when the older boy had to mow the lawn. Stan Freeze-Framed his overcare and realized why it was okay for the older boy to have more chores. He was at a different developmental level and more able than the younger boy. Stan released his overcare and with sincere care explained the reason to the boys. Fewer rules and explanations are needed as family members experience heart perception with each other. Heart perception creates entrainment — being in sync with each other.

The outright nature of parenthood imparts power over children. Lawfully, parents are responsible for a child's behavior and well-being. Society reinforces this power of authority. If a child damages a neighbor's property, the parents are legally liable. If a parent neglects his child's health and safety, there are laws to remove a child from parental custody. As a child relies on a parent for physical and emotional needs, the child is bestowed with one of life's greatest treasures: an authority figure.

Common sense involves perceiving a child's qualifications for rational and heart intelligent action. The heart intelligent parent grants power in areas where the child has shown responsibility but limits power where the child has not. A child may be allowed to answer the telephone if she has shown that she speaks politely, clearly, and is responsible to convey messages. That same child may not be mature enough to stay at home alone with a friend while the parent goes to the store.

The heart approach to discipline requires continuously trying to find the balance. Children require solid parents who care enough to become interested. The balanced heart approach is real care. As you practice the HeartMath tools, you will develop your own common-sense discipline methods. Each individual, each parent, each family, has to decide within their own hearts what form of discipline works best for each child.

The child raised in an overpermissive atmosphere views her parents as unsound. Running her parents around can produce anxiety and guilt in the child. I've heard many children confess, *"My folks let me do whatever I wanted. I could leave the house for hours and not have to tell my folks where I was going. I could disobey my dad and watch TV shows he said I couldn't and he wouldn't do anything about it. It made me feel I wasn't worth caring about. My parents should have made me mind."* This is a cry for care.

When you engineer a heart-filled environment, you cultivate an atmosphere to meet a child's physical, emotional, and mental needs. All children need space to stretch out, play, and be physically active. They need a yard or open area that is safe to explore, climb, dig, splash, holler, and run, without damaging valuable property. If you live in confined quarters, create the time and place where your children can freely explore, such as a playground or park. Choose toys and rules that meet your child's emotional needs. Some parents expect five year olds to embrace complex challenges. If you give your four year old tiny Lego® blocks for building instead of bigger Duplo® blocks, and he doesn't have the small motor skill coordination to assemble them easily, he'll feel frustrated. Or if you give him rules more suited to a ten year old, such as allowing him to stay up until 9:30 on school nights because he says he's not tired, you're likely to have a cranky child.

Children need to ask questions. If parents frequently show impatience or are too busy to answer their questions, it stifles mental development. Many parents recognize the importance of spending "quality" time with children. There is a tremendous difference between *heart quality time* and *head quantity time*. If you spend thirty minutes with a child and your head is distracted with work, the football game on TV, or phone interruptions, your time with your child has little value. Quality comes from the heart. With heart quality, read a story, play a game, answer questions, or discuss topics your child is interested in to encourage creative thinking.

Heart quality time creates bonding and deepens communication. It balances discipline. These are all examples to help you engineer an expanding, but safe and secure, quality atmosphere. It is essential that family rules be clear-cut, emotionally embraceable, and fair to all. Discipline is a must to ensure peaceful family existence. Evaluate your discipline — does it create security and strengthen your child? Does your discipline structure make the entire family stronger and more secure? Does it add heart hope to your family? If not, utilize your heart intelligence to make needed adjustments.

Balanced Discipline

Many parents use restriction as a form of discipline. If you confine a child to the house or to her room and then allow her to entertain herself with TV, video games, or heavy metal music, the grounding may have little effect. Other parents use "time-out" as a method of discipline. Isolation time-out, in balance, can be effective. But if time-out means sitting on a bench watching other children or playing alone with toys, the child is distracted and not necessarily reflecting on the rule she has broken.

An effective heart approach to discipline is putting children "on the wall." A child stands facing a wall in a quiet place for a specific length of time. Younger children sit on a chair facing the wall. "The Wall" gives a child time to slow down and really ponder the rule he has broken *without distractions*. First talk to the child, speaking truth from the heart so he understands why he's being put on the wall. Then ask him to spend the wall time pondering — from the heart — what he did. Have him practice FREEZE-FRAME to help his intuitive understanding. While on the wall, no one speaks to the child, nor is the child allowed to talk. When time-out is over, you can have a calm, heart-to-heart talk with the child. Ask him what he has learned about the situation. Practice the INTUITIVE LISTENING tool and speak your truth.

Sometimes it may be important to remove privileges as a method of discipline, such as taking away a toy or not allowing a child to go somewhere. The heart approach allows you to remove privileges consciously and with balance. Banning use of electronics, such as movies, TV, and video games for a designated period of time, is also an effective form of discipline. Electronics can easily overstimulate head frequencies, creating imbalances that make it harder for a child to connect with the heart. Listening too much to music on a CD player or tape recorder can do the same. When you remove electronics, help your child find balance in opposite activities. Give him books to read, talk to him more, or play with him outdoors.

Once you identify a behavior that needs to be changed, use your heart intuition to decide which balanced discipline would be best for your child. Lay out the rule and the consequence if it is broken. For example: Your child has been playing outside late. Set the time you want him to be home, say 8:50 p.m. Tell him, *"I would like you home at 8:50 p.m. each night. If you are home after 9:00 p.m., the consequence will be you can't play outside after supper for one week."* By giving him ten minutes latitude between the time you want him home and the time the consequence goes into effect, you respect that a child might need to finish a play if he's in the middle of a soccer game, or use the restroom before he comes home. Balanced discipline provides a firm bottom-line and appropriate latitude that respects a child and the flows of life. Here's another example: One of your daughter's chores is to wash the dishes after dinner. Often she forgets to do them and has to be reminded. Sometimes she leaves them piled in the sink for hours, then washes them hurriedly and doesn't get them totally clean. Tell her, *"I would like the dishes completely washed by 8:00 p.m. each night. If there is a TV show you want to watch or some reason you need to do them later, you have to first get my permission and the new time by which they will be done. If the dishes aren't done on time, you will not be able to watch TV for three days."* Again, your consequence allows for some flexibility while maintaining a firm bottom-line. You can apply this same balanced discipline to other areas, such as cleaning her room, taking out the garbage, feeding the dog, earning her allowance, etc.

If you really love your children, you will discipline them and you will set firm bottom-lines, rules, and boundaries. The heart approach creates a common-sense joint venture between head and heart. It's just business, the business of raising a child in the high-stressed '90s and beyond. Practice the HeartMath tools described in this manual. They have proven effective for many parents, children, and families. Observe and listen to your children to first understand how they perceive. Then speak your truth from the heart. Stay a street ahead and guide children with heart intelligence. Demonstrate how to develop

Chapter 8

The Beginning Patterns Of Growth

When does parenting begin? At the biological level, it all starts with the DNA. What role do DNA and heredity play in parenting? The parents' sperm and ovum unite, combining DNA information. As the human embryo develops, cells organize and arrange themselves in the body according to the genetic blueprint contained within the DNA in each cell. The DNA has all the data and know-how necessary to grow a child. It contains the code of life. There is something in DNA that would inspire a sixteen year old to say, *"I think existence is an incredible thing, an incredible unfathomable miracle, like magic. Its beauty is in that it can be incredibly wonderful or incredibly terrible and everything in between and it's good. I don't know what the meaning of life is, but the value of life, what makes it worthwhile is love — if you live without love, you are not really living."*

Science has known for years that physical qualities are genetically determined. Often we hear someone say, "He looks just like his dad! He has the same stature, the same eyes, the same nose, the resemblance is amazing!" Human DNA contains twenty-three pairs of chromosomes. Each chromosome contains millions of genes, and each gene is responsible for one hereditary factor, such as eye color, bone structure, height, baldness, color-blindness, etc. Many common diseases have their origins in chromosomal or genetic abnormalities, such as Down's syndrome, cystic fibrosis, hemophilia, and sickle-cell anemia.

The temperament and personality traits of a child also have genetically determined factors. Genetics influence our brain chemistry and neurological development. Similar psychological characteristics between parent and child also have inherited biological components. For example, child and parent can have similar tendencies, such as excessive worrying, timidity, leadership qualities, risk-taking, obedience to authority, etc. My mother is fun-loving and a risk taker. I have these same qualities. An employee on the IHM staff, Richard, was separated from his father when he was one and a half years old. He and his father met again and spent time together when Richard was forty-four. They were amazed at their similarities which were certainly not due to environmental influence. Both are very service-oriented and like to care for people. Both are musicians. Both are avid readers and love to travel. Both are driven over-achievers; if they don't do something perfectly, they tend to judge themselves harshly.

Ask your parents what you were like as a child. Were your personality characteristics similar to one of your parents? Do you see parallel virtues or weaknesses? It's part of nature's program. Inheritance plays a key role in personality development, but not the entire role. Although DNA prescribes tendencies, people still have opportunities to learn different behaviors.

How does the DNA know what to do? From where does this marvelous intelligence originate? In the book, *Embraced by the Light*, Betty J. Eadie describes her profound near-death experience where she was given an understanding of the spiritual or etheric aspect of the DNA blueprint.[12] Read by millions of people eager to understand the meaning of life, her book was #1 on the *New York Times* bestseller list. Betty suggests that in the spirit world before birth, people are aware of the genetic coding and particular features they will have in their human bodies. They select their blueprint on Earth for certain evolutionary, learning experiences. I have had experiences similar to Betty's, although their truth cannot be scientifically verified as yet. Betty describes aspects of the spiritual blueprint as follows: *" . . . All thoughts and experiences are recorded in our subconscious minds. They are also recorded in our cells, so that, not only is each cell imprinted with a genetic coding, it is also imprinted with every experience we have had. Further, I understood that these memories are passed down through the genetic coding to our children. These memories then account for many of the passed-on traits in families, such as addictive tendencies, fears, strengths, and so on."* But she adds, *"If you could see yourself before you were born, you would be amazed at your intelligence and glory."*

The child's spirit begins, from birth through seven years old, to learn about physical forms and principles. Meeting with a mother's nipple is a comfort to an infant. For the first few weeks of a baby's life, the mouth is the number one conduit of perception. It is a communicational sense organ; from day one, babies spit, drool, cry, babble, and gurgle. At first, the baby breastfeeds with eyes shut tight because she cannot handle more than one activity at a time. As the infant expands information intake, she can feed and see. Infants easily feel when a parent is radiating love to them. Their hearts respond to that loving, radiant energy. It feels good to them and they often radiate that love back to you naturally. The communicational feedback of smiling and cooing starts at about five weeks of life. These inborn designs are instincts. All children of all cultures follow similar body developments and mature at an equivalent rate. Compared to other species, human babies have a long, slow development toward autonomy.

Natural Laws and Human Growth

Physics has observed and validated the existence of many natural laws of energy, motion, and force. Einstein discovered and mathematically proved that $E=mc^2$, which means that energy and matter are equivalent. This led to Quantum theory which mandates that physical events and subjective consciousness form a unified system — therefore everything is made of energy vibrating at different frequencies, including sensory input, thoughts, and feelings. Babies begin exploring these different frequencies from day one. A baby can focus her attention on a particular object or frequency she sees or hears, amidst a bombardment of stimulation.

Entrainment is a phenomenon seen throughout nature where systems or organisms sync up in order to work at maximum efficiency. It's the Law of Conservation of Energy — nature's way of operating at highest efficiency. Flocks of birds entrain to fly in formation. A room full of pendulum clocks will entrain to the rhythm of the largest pendulum and swing in unison. An infant at her mother's breast will initially have a heart rhythm different from the mother's, but in a small amount of time, the infant's system adjusts to the heart rhythm of the mother so that the two hearts entrain to the same rhythm.

There is an unspoken knowingness (an intuitive entrainment) between mother and child. An infant can be fussing in a room far from the mother's hearing, yet the mother knows the baby is in need. An inner feeling tells her to check on the baby and more often than not the signal is right. When she appears, the child is gratified. Through love, she intuitively answers many subtle cues from the baby. If a mother is under stress, the feeling of love can be negated. This blocks the intuitive link. The more stress a mother is under, the more she will miscue. Love can re-establish the intuitive connection so parent and child communicate with maximum efficiency. If the primary caretaker is the father or someone besides the natural mother, the blueprint is changed through the caretaker's love. Many parents who have adopted babies confirm there is an intuitive process of linking with the baby's deeper nature. You can help your infant identify love as a warm, radiant feeling that comes from the heart. This will nurture the intuitive bond between you. Sincerely spend time with and love your infant.

An infant may suffer from colic or crying spells the mother can't assuage. Sending love to a baby is soothing and helps both mother and child relax. It gives the mother something positive to do. A friend described her experience with her four-month-old son. *"I would rock my baby, drive him around in the car, try anything to take his colic away, but nothing worked. His cries of pain would about drive me crazy because there was nothing I could do. Radiating love to him and practicing the HeartMath tools helped the most. It kept my sanity."* When a mother feels helpless and frustrated, it actually makes it harder on both mother and baby. An infant feels both his own pain and his mother's tension.

Since babies are very sensitive to energies, they intuitively sense when you are changing your energy. An infant will begin to notice your shift in mood and energy when you are Freeze-Framing. As they feel you relax and your stress release, they often respond in a positive way. A baby may stop grunting with frustration and start squealing with excitement because you shifted the energy in the room. To teach a young baby to naturally FREEZE-FRAME begins with being an example.

Children's early muscular body movements unfold and evolve into the fine and gross motor skills. Their spirits are propelled to physically interact with the Earth. A baby can hold her head up at about four months which permits spacious visual capacity. Babies can clearly differentiate distances while reaching for objects. Your baby begins to sit and balance at six months old. Bodily movements and sensory experiences form patterns in the baby's new brain cells. The attempt to sit up makes an attempted pattern in the baby's brain. Through repeated efforts, the baby etches in these brain patterns more securely.

During the second half of the first year of life, a baby will learn and perfect fundamental skills to exist and express in this world. Her capabilities expand at seven months — pushing up on her hands and knees, rocking back and forth as she creeps forward. Soon your baby will be crawling, exploring everything. Distinguishing family members and saying "dada" or "mama" is a sheer delight. As you love your baby, she may become more peaceful, smile, hold out her arms, or perhaps reach to hug you when she feels this radiance.

By nine months a baby has refined his sitting and crawling skills. The baby establishes a specific crawling pattern as his speed advances. Pulling up on furniture or grasping a hand, he soon learns to balance. Slowly the baby is growing conscious of the vertical axis. As he reaches the twelve month mark, he is actively exploring from various viewpoints. He is now acknowledging social expression, and loves to have parents' approval and applause for his accomplishments. As you practice radiating sincere feelings of love to your baby, you will develop a more secure intuitive understanding of how to teach your baby. In a loving atmosphere, a baby feels more sure taking on challenges in his motor skill expansion.

Young children are very sensitive to a parent who is worried, insecure, or emotionally disturbed. They may identify with your feelings and take them on as their own. A worried parent often begets a worried child. Or, in self-protection, a child may recoil from a worried or insecure parent and gravitate toward the more secure parent. Remember, children learn how to perceive from their parents. As you FREEZE-FRAME and shift perception and mood, infants and young children feel your worries release and become happier.

When a child ages zero to seven still seems worried, upset, hurt, insecure, or anxious, hold him in your lap as you practice the HeartMath tools. Ask him to put the problem in his heart and stir it around in there, like stirring soup or blending chocolate in milk. You can pretend you have a spoon in your hand and gently stir the energy around your child's heart as you love your child. An infant is tuned to the heart and will feel the energy stirring and blending. Sincerely feel love and care (not overcare please) for your child. After a few moments say, "Now, let's relax and soak, like we're in a nice heart-warming bath." Teaching an infant or toddler how to find their heart and relax while in a real, nice warm bath or bubble bath can be very soothing and helpful. You will sense when your child releases the worry or anxiety. He will become more relaxed and peaceful. In some children, you can see a new sparkle in their eyes or they look lighter and more playful.

One Year Old

As I discuss general development patterns for each year, realize each child is different and may not display every characteristic described.

Most babies start to walk by the end of the first year, but this new independence can be overwhelming at times for a toddler. He may balk at parting from his mother or have childlike anxieties about being left with an unknown baby sitter. For the most part, the one year old toddler is exceptionally curious and lovable. In a loving field of energy, he adjusts smoothly to whatever his mother's persuasion may be. As your toddler progresses through this year, his locomotive abilities expand, his capacity to grasp and maneuver objects heighten, and his gestures of vocabulary increase. Toddlers love to investigate and feel all things; this is their way of exploring Earth. As toddlers expand and evolve, they learn more of the physical principles of Earth, the natural laws by which the Earth operates.

A natural law toddlers explore is the Law of Gravity which states that gravity is a force that acts on every material thing. Because of the Earth's enormous mass, its gravitational force is so strong that any object is pulled to the ground. The closer to the ground, the stronger the pull. An example to a toddler: If you fall down, you go boom. Children learn that wind will blow leaves around and air currents will carry a helium balloon high into the sky, but everything eventually falls to the ground.

Two Years Old

By age two, you can begin teaching a child how to lock-in to the heart feeling of love and radiate it to mommy, daddy, sisters, broth-

113

ers, pets, teddy bears, friends, grandparents, and so forth. Start by putting your hand on your own heart or his heart and explain that's the place where people feel love. Love's abundance is locked in your heart until you take a key and open it, and send it to someone. You can play a game where you each put your palm on the heart to send love to people you know. As a parent knowing and understanding your toddler, you will have creative games of your own to play. The second year of a toddler's life draws him to participate more fully with Earth's realities: nature, creatures, objects, facts, and events. The typical two year old's physical skills are more stable. Emotionally your toddler will seem more composed, serene, and easygoing as life is no longer as frustrating for him. Frequently he will express himself by stating his name and what he wants. As he phrases his demands, he will also conclude that the object is, "Mine!" This is part of growth, so parents understand and show him how, "This is mine, but I like to share," and then also show him, "This is mommy's purse, but this blanket is yours." A two year old likes having things clearly defined. He prefers the same schedule every day, in the same sequence, which allows him to feel solid and secure. It's not always possible for busy parents to provide a regular defined schedule. To make it easier for your two year old, explain any anticipated schedule change two days ahead of time when possible, then remind him several times in a fun way that it's coming. This will help him feel prepared. A two year old would love to play a FREEZE-FRAME game at various scheduled times each day. It helps him learn to calm down and feel secure.

A FREEZE-FRAME Game for Toddlers

When you close your eyes and put your hand on your heart as you FREEZE-FRAME, your child will become curious as she feels the shift in energy. Tell your toddler you are Freeze-Framing and taking a time-out. Children at this age learn by imitating parents. This will also help her start to understand that "time-out" is for the purpose of managing your energies and getting back into the heart. Freeze-Framing is not just a discipline for poor behavior. It's a tool to help you feel better. As soon as a child is old enough to play patty-cake, around age two, play a FREEZE-FRAME game that goes like this.

When you say "FREEZE-FRAME" everyone stops still. Move around, dance, clap, sing, then say "FREEZE-FRAME." Everyone puts their hand on their heart and freezes all motion and sound. A toddler can learn that Freeze-Framing means stop, be still, and be quiet as a mouse.

Soon your toddler will move into a phase our society has defined as "The Terrible Twos." It varies for each toddler, but frequently it is two and a half years old when this difficult expression appears. The drastic change to the terrible twos can startle a parent. The child turns inflexible and uptight almost instantly. His high-rise emotions explode with intense demands. What's happening at this stage? A toddler constructs antitheses, investigating two opposite limits in rapid sequence, exploring the Law of Cause and Effect. Some examples of opposites are, today he loves apples, tomorrow he hates them and wants an orange; this minute he wants mom's help, the next he wants to do it himself or demands dad's help. He sets up the same formalities each day to elude the tug-of-war of having to make a choice. He is so confused by choices he demands everything the same. He has many temper tantrums when he can't have his own way. At this age he may speak in sentences to communicate what he does want or does not want. The terrible twos reflect a child's effort to develop his own will. However, it does not have to be a period when his will dominates the entire family.

The editor of this book used the tools provided in *A Parenting Manual* to address the needs of her two and a half year old who was out of control, running everyone around. He purposely threw food on the floor (and many other actions) or purposely dined like a gentleman to see how his mother would react. The mother didn't want to squelch his spirit and didn't know what to do. In doing HEART LOCK-INs and practicing the tools, the mother realized she could help the boy by showing him the opposite of what she'd been doing, in a business-like, but loving way. The next time he acted out, instead of trying to pacify him, she was firm and let him know that disrespectful behavior was not allowed. She did it again and again until the boy knew what was permitted and what was not. At first the child was surprised. Then he kept looking for cues from his mother, wondering what was going on. She kept listening to her intuition for guidance and maintained a firm bottom-line for one month. After a month the boy's behavior totally changed; he understood opposites and was a joy to be around. A heart intelligent parent attunes to the child and aids him in adjusting the radical and intense behavior. As you develop your skills at Freeze-Framing, you will intuitively discover ways to teach your child opposites through the challenging times, without him going to as many extremes.

Three Years Old

As your child leaves the terrible twos there will be much less resistance, for her growth doesn't need so many creative challenges. The three year old child feels confident in her abilities. She is more physically assured, emotionally tranquil, and mentally lighthearted. She loves her new usage of communication. By age three she can name people she wants to send love to each day. Parent and child can play a fun game where you recall special experiences you've had together where you felt warm, radiant love, care, or appreciation. The attention span is extending so this is a prime time for parents to communicate with their child. When you teach your three year old to say "please" and "thank you," teach her to send heart sincerely as she speaks these words, rather than just speak a required courtesy.

With a three year old's increased smoothness in motor skills, she loves to play outside. A toddler can be given the structure of her fenced-in backyard to play. She has freedom to play with any toys, but can't go outside the yard. The yard is the frame within which the child has flexibility to put the puzzle of life together. Define the structures, then allow your child choice within that framework.

A three year old can skillfully use the pedals to ride a tricycle. As the child learns to ride, she starts to explore the first Law of Motion which states: Acceleration is proportional to force and constant force produces constant acceleration. A child on wheels soon discovers if you push the pedals too fast, you might not be able to control the ride.

As the third year moves on, friends become meaningful. Three year old play displays imagination, creativity, and the ability to interact. He increasingly becomes aware of others' reactions. A three year old might say, "I love you, Mommy," attuned to your feelings. Hug him and notice how your child responds to your love. Affirm the love as he expresses his affection. Frequently between routines and during playtime, he is entertaining and enjoying himself. There are times where life does not go his way and he reacts with a sudden burst of tears. But with love he can be flexible and quickly turn back to joyful play.

Four Years Old

Four year olds express themselves from their most centered beingness. In her heart she can love a lot; in her head she can scream a lot. If parents comprehend their four year old child from a heart perspective, she is quite a dynamic little person. If a parent does not comprehend her, then she is seemingly domineering and overbearing. A four year old is so elated to express herself, she is willing to do whatever. Physically, her motor skills burst into high gear and likewise her emotions. She behaves securely with new speculations, concepts, and perceptions. A four year old can enthrall parents with heart words of wisdom. Then playing on a parent's attentive response, instantly go to the head and keep on talking to hold the parent's attention or to manipulate the parent into getting what she wants. Four year old Shawna, looking up at the clear sky one day exclaimed, "Oh look, look, the sun and moon are both up at the same time! I want to go to the moon. I love life. I love you so much mommy. Isn't life wonderful?" Her captivated mother answered, "Yes it is, darling." As Shawna noticed how impressed her mother was, she continued talking but from the head, "Mom, you know you're the best mom in the whole wide world, you take such good care of me, you make my food, and take me places. Mommy, can we go to the park, then can we get pizza for supper tonight? Can we? I love pizza." Parents need to encourage a child's moments of wisdom, then also help them create balance.

Because of her exuberant self, a four year old can turn blatantly irate within seconds. When small children are angry, it is best not to intervene unless to prevent harm or to remove them from the room if they are disturbing others. Allow a heated episode to play itself out. As the child becomes manageable again, review the experience with her to assist the child's understanding. When four year old Bryan had a temper tantrum, any effort to intervene inflamed him to hit, pinch, and become violent. It's better to leave the temper tantrum alone and not add extra fuel.

Practice FREEZE-FRAME together when your child is peaceful and happy. Then explain that Freeze-Framing also helps children and adults take "time-out" to feel better when they are upset, cranky, hurt, or angry, and that it's fun to practice at those times too. When a child is upset, help her take a time-out and use her FREEZE-FRAME tool. Then discuss the situation.

As a child approaches five, he is seemingly more self-motivated. While in his heart, there can be endless questions of how and why in his quest for knowledge. While in his head, there can be never ending, "Why do I have to?" or "How come?" in resistance. At this age, most are sincerely on a quest for knowledge, but sometimes they just like to hear themselves talk. Use your intelligence to discriminate. Children love to talk to teddy bears, dolls, animals, nature, etc., about themselves, their families, their stresses, and why they feel worried. So, naturally children would love to FREEZE-FRAME and learn how to talk to their own heart.

Teaching FREEZE-FRAME —
Age Four to Six

By age four, a child can learn that FREEZE-FRAME means stop your mind and put your thoughts on "pause." Show a child what happens when you "pause" a movie on TV by pressing the pause button on your VCR. The picture and sound freeze. Explain that's what we're doing inside when we FREEZE-FRAME. Then teach him the steps.

Step 1. Explain how Freeze-Framing is pausing his body and thoughts.

Step 2. Explain that the next step is to let all his thoughts stream down into his heart. Then place your hand on his heart.

Step 3. Tell him, "Feel the warmness of your heart washing all the thoughts away."

Step 4. Then say, "Now take a minute to feel your heart and remember someone you love." Pause a few seconds.

Step 5. Continue by saying, "Now ask your heart to tell you what would make you feel better or what you need to do. Remember, your heart is very smart and has good answers that can help you and other people too."

Step 6. Ask the child, "Sincerely listen to your heart. What is it saying to you?"

Step 7. Help your child do what his heart is saying.

Five and Six Years Old

As children reach the ages of five and six, they are growing more mature and responsible. They are beginning to separate from their mothers and step into being an integral part of the family unit. They can try so hard to be independent that it causes them much stress. Again and again, they can hesitate, be indecisive, and have a hard time making choices. At this age, a child's brain cells are expanding rapidly so life feels difficult. He has less control of his motor skills, and emotionally he seems like he is having continuous stress. He can seem so awkward and anxious. If he's in his head, he can be quite demanding, even sassy. This is because he is so eager to be accepted and loved that he cannot stand failure. Lovingly lead him back to the heart, then he is a joy. Five and six year olds love new experiences, new thoughts, new understandings, and have increased academic capabilities. Understand that his reality is rapidly changing. Frequently, he will try to re-construct himself by only doing the things he knows how. Help him FREEZE-FRAME and find his inner resources. Aid him in new challenges, as he dearly loves his family and needs enormous support and reassurance from them.

Typical five and six year olds love to communicate. Being a heart-intelligent parent, take advantage of this particular age to establish solid communication skills. Read him books, talk to him, ask questions, and tell him stories and facts. Deep heart listen and speak your truth. At this age, a child loves modeling himself after his parents. Here is a fun "Deep Heart Listening and Speak Your Truth" game to play with five and six year olds.

Deep Heart Listening and Speak Your Truth

Step 1. One person is the "Communicator" and the other the "Listener." Communicator, name three things you loved this week — about something, or someone, or loved about yourself. Remember times you *felt* love. Family members can help the "Communicator" pick the times. Examples might be: sitting on grandpa's knee, loving your new shoes, laughing with your best friend, etc.

Step 2. Communicator, tell the Listener how those special times made you feel. Speak sincerely from your heart. Imagine there is a mouth sitting right inside your heart, with the lips moving as you are talking. (Speak one or two short sentences at a time.)

Step 3. Listener needs to listen from the heart too. Imagine there is an ear sitting right inside your heart. This will help you listen more deeply. Deep heart listening means to listen without your own thoughts running around in your mind at the same time. If thoughts come up, simply love them and let them go (don't fight them), then bring your attention back to the ear in your heart so you can listen more deeply to what the Communicator is saying behind the words. *Send love as you listen.*

Step 4. When the Communicator is finished, then the Listener must say back (like a mirror) what you heard the Communicator say to be sure you heard it right. Now it's the Listener's turn to imagine there's a mouth talking from his heart. The Listener mirrors until the Communicator agrees that he feels heard and understood. Other family members can help coach, but they have to listen too.

Step 5. It's now the Listener's turn to tell about three things he loved this week. Switch roles and go through the four steps again.

If children have wandering attention while they are learning to Deep Heart Listen, play FREEZE-FRAME. Everyone freeze for a moment, stop, and shift to the heart. Now look at each other. Now listen again. Don't interrupt each other. Wait until it is your turn to speak.

Before seven years old, children are not qualified for self-discipline. It is illogical for a parent to count upon a six year old to have the abstract thinking necessary to control their feelings and make certain logical choices. As age seven begins, intellectual challenges become fun, creative resistances. A seven year old's ability for enjoyment of her own accomplishments are monumental. The child has now shaped her life from birth to seven and is ready to move into logical thought.

Chapter 9

The Middle Years
of Childhood

From ages seven to twelve, a child assembles perceptions from the father, the family, and the world. The mother's close relationship with the child changes at about age seven, but continues with the same depth of love through the intuitional field. This is loving from a distance, allowing the child to grow without excessive parenting. Some mothers have a hard time releasing their seven year olds. Mothers tend to cling when they haven't developed an inner knowing of when to provide protection and security and when to let go.

At age seven, the child starts to develop her own unique perceptions, thoughts, and ideas. As her sense of self-governing progresses, she is physically secure with the basic principles and laws of the physical world. She can consider advancing freely into complex thought. By the age of seven, the primary self-language system is complete. Research indicates that a brain growth spurt occurs during the sixth year of age. By seven, children have four to five times more neural connections in the brain than they had at eighteen months. The DNA blueprint unfoldment now introduces intellect and more individualized perception.

Children at seven years old start to understand relationships. They explore natural laws of magnetism, attraction, and repulsion in relationships. They are conscious of people they like and don't like. At the age of seven, children begin to understand simple mathematical reasoning. They already know 1+1=2 and now can understand abstractly that adding and subtracting increases or reduces the total number. They're able to use logical reasoning and heart intelligence in solving problems as challenges. These challenges involve both interacting with concrete objects and experiencing events.

During the years eight to ten, the child begins to develop a sense of his personal self. He is expanding the theoretical and becoming competent in dealing with the hypothetical. Let's say he's asked, "What if the teacher gives you extra homework due tomorrow, but you have a soccer game after school and a movie you are planning to watch in the evening?" A ten year old can use complex thought to consider several possible answers and suggest appropriate responses. He is also learning to discriminate various concepts regarding feelings. An example would be sincerely comprehending what an adult means by the question, "How will that boy feel about you calling him names?" A younger child may say, "I don't know," or "He'll feel bad," because he's been told so. A ten year old would be able to feel and understand the feelings of the other child.

Discovering Individuality

Individuality is a child's accumulation of perceptions about himself in the world as he grows. It's through these accumulations that he acquires values, absolutes, and various thought and feeling patterns. The perception process develops as an automatic result of commonsense abilities. Young children learn about physical opposites, such as black or white, up or down, inside or outside. They progress to learning abstract opposites about what is fair or unfair, lawful or unlawful. For example, children are often told, "Letting everyone take a turn playing a game is fair." They quickly feel and know that, "Letting everyone but me take a turn is unfair." However, understanding, "Letting everyone take a turn except the kid you don't like is also unfair," requires another frame in commonsense perception.

Children who do not progress through all these stages of perception may not be able to differentiate appropriately when they are teenagers, and therefore think there is nothing inappropriate in singling out another child for ridicule, rejection, or harm. They are unable to understand the real meaning of commonsense qualities, attitudes, and values. They may use words like truth and compassion, without grasping the meaning of these heart concepts. Understanding mathematical abstractions based on qualitative values like a+b=c instead of quantitative values is also difficult for them.

Starting at age seven, life begins to expand both internally within a child's concepts and externally in her reality. In her new understanding of individuality, a creative relationship occurs between the two intelligence systems — the head and the heart. This unfoldment changes the internal information structure which determines how a child perceives. Concepts begin to be constructed out of imaginative ideas or possibilities concerning the world. A hard intellectual problem can demonstrate a challenge rather than cause the frustration it previously had. A child expands her idea of herself through interactions with family, friends, school, and the community.

Understanding Your Seven to Twelve Year Old's Perceptions

As a child progresses, he increasingly grows into a person shaped by his perceptions. His perceptions are the key to what he is, what he does, and in which direction his life will turn. However, a child often bases his perceptions and behavior on how he *thinks* his parents' perceive him. If a child perceives he gets criticized every time he makes a mess trying to help, he feels incapable. He may start to judge himself harshly, misbehave, or throw temper tantrums. The parents' perception is often that they're just trying to teach him to do things right. Failing to understand the child's perspective, their ongoing frustrations can cause the child's self-judgments and irrational behavior. The parent unknowingly could be creating a stressful environment. As parents try to change a child's *behavior* without first changing the child's *perception*, the child becomes increasingly confused, judgmental, and adamant.

To understand your child at any stage, step back and observe — see from your child's eyes without your own assumptions. Ask yourself, "How is my child perceiving this situation?" Listen to your intuition. Only then will you know in which direction to steer him. Through the heart a child can change his perceptions easily because his perceptions have not yet been carved in stone.

From age seven to twelve, your child can understand at a deeper level what radiating or sending heart energy means. Explain how love radiates warmth from your heart, just like light radiates warmth from a light bulb, or like the sun radiates warmth to the whole world. Discuss how loving people helps you understand them better. By sending heart to someone, your heart can help you find new thoughts and new ways to be friends or help them. Do it with him, especially if he is having a problem with someone and wants to send heart to find some new solutions. Then talk about what you both felt and any new thoughts you had. Explain how these positive new thoughts are intuition from the heart. This still small voice inside will be his best friend for life.

Seven to twelve is significantly a thinking age. If parents observe carefully, they will see their children alternate between periods of expansion and contraction. In the contraction phase, a child may be introverted. Even a very extroverted child has quiet times inside himself. Children are effectively guided if heart-intelligent parents keep in mind the inner subtleties and complexities going on. They are gathering massive amounts of information, acquiring knowledge on how to perceive life.

For children, a sense of belonging and a belief in themselves are essential for healthy development. Throughout this age range, a child characterizes himself by looking outside the family. This magnifies a focus on peers, so friends have a multiplying influence. The transition to a peer focus is not intended to dispose of parents. In fact, family remains the chief influence for deeper attitudes. Friends influence modes of expression, clothes, words, etc. They also affect attitude, but more on a surface level. For example, a child whose parents model and instill a sincere respect for others is less prone to imitating a friend's disrespectful behavior. However, how peers view him might color his perception. If peers expect a friend to act as they do, he could oblige. He might try out the disrespectful behavior, but if deeper heart values have been ingrained it won't feel comfortable. The resulting inner conflict compels him to self-correct or, if peer confirmation has become more important, to rebel. Peers are frequently a child's prime source of communication today. Peers signify those who have a similar level of age, insight, and knowledge. If children speak predominantly with peers, they lack exposure to people with more skills and developed mental and emotional abilities.

Teaching Seven to Twelve Year Olds How to FREEZE-FRAME

Between seven and twelve, the effort at establishing selfhood can feel overwhelming. Responsible, conscious choice is a heart-empowered skill and to develop this children can practice FREEZE-FRAME. From ages seven to twelve, children want to understand how everything works, including Freeze-Framing. They can understand the purpose of Freeze-Framing, how it works, and use the tool on their own.

Preliminary Steps that Facilitate Teaching
FREEZE-FRAME — Age Seven to Twelve

Step 1. First explain the difference between the head and the heart. Discuss how you use your head to memorize, read words, do arithmetic, and think. You use your heart to feel feelings, like care, appreciation, laughter, fun, joy, and love. Without having a heart to feel good and enjoy things in life, living isn't fun.

Step 2. Ask your child to name people, places and things she appreciates, like favorite relatives, friends, foods, colors, cartoon characters, places, movies. This helps children see they have a wealth of positive experiences and feelings to draw upon. Your child can also write this appreciation list on small blank cards or pieces of paper.

Step 3. Next ask your child to name or write a list of things about herself and her own life that she appreciates. Help her understand that people feel appreciation in the heart.

Step 4. Then discuss how FREEZE-FRAME allows you to feel the power of your own heart, the power of your own love, care, and appreciation.

There are two other preliminary steps I use prior to teaching a child age seven to twelve how to FREEZE-FRAME. I ask the child what he does when he gets upset or when someone is bothering him. Does he ignore it, get mad, tell the person to stop it, or leave? I then explain these are all little steps, but there's another response or tool that can really help in the moment. It's based on the power of your heart. Using the tool FREEZE-FRAME allows you to *feel* the power of your own heart and have it work for you.

It's important to ask children to "feel the heart" as it is so easy for them to try Freeze-Framing mechanically from the head when they are stuck in anger, being upset, arguing, or going fast. Then I explain that you FREEZE-FRAME by shifting from your head to your heart. Imagine a leaf falling in a zigzag pattern from a tree limb to the ground. Move your hand from head to heart to illustrate. That's what it's like switching from the head to the heart. A visual, moving image for this shift is important for children because it appeals to the kinesthetic and visual learning modalities. Sometimes a falling snowflake is a helpful initial image.

In teaching Freeze-Framing, you first need to walk children through each of the steps and answer any questions. Pick a time when you can have a quiet talk about things that bother him and things he appreciates, and discuss these preliminary steps.

Once she has learned the tool, you can help your child apply the tool when she is upset or angry. I tell the child, *"It sounds like you are (or were) angry because things weren't going your way. Let's FREEZE-FRAME and go to the heart and see if we can find a better solution."* In the beginning, it takes a little coaching. Sometimes you have to re-mind her that she is not listening and is off in her mind not paying attention or arguing, and that's not her true heart. I tell her, *"Your true heart can help you find a better solution. Let's find it."* So you help a child acknowledge her stressful feeling and take time-out. That's Step 1.

For Step 2, I tell the child, *"Now in a relaxed way, we can listen to each other. I know you're angry. With FREEZE-FRAME you let go of those angry feelings and focus on your true heart. Put your hand on your heart, and pretend that you're breathing through your heart to help you feel your heart. Let's do it for ten seconds. I'll time you."* Children enjoy being timed. It's a fun game that helps them focus on the heart and FREEZE-FRAME more sincerely.

For Step 3, I say, *"Now, remember a time when you felt truly happy.*

Maybe you were with your mother, or playing with a friend or with a pet. Appreciate that for ten seconds. You can close your eyes if you'd like. I'll time you."

After ten seconds are up, I go to Step 4, and say, *"Now, sincerely ask your heart, what would be a better way for you to respond to the problem you were having, something that can help you and the other person? Listen to your heart . . . (Pause) What is your heart saying?"*

In Step 5, I listen to the child's answer. Sometimes it's helpful to repeat back to the child what he tells you, and ask if you heard him correctly. This helps him feel acknowledged. If his heart has given an appropriate answer, tell him you think that's a good idea and help him follow through with it. If the answer is not appropriate, ask him if that would really work, or be best for both him and the other person. Guide the child to his sincere, honest heart feelings. You will be helping him understand his own intuitive intelligence and soon he will be able to apply Freeze-Framing on his own in life situations.

If an older child tempts an eight year old to take drugs, the younger child will say "no" because his parents told him that's what he's supposed to do. A twelve year old is capable of saying "no" based on understanding the possible future consequences. Children can develop heart intelligence to concentrate on hypothetical questions and unfold a knowledge of cause and effect to assist in finding effective answers. By seven years old, a child really can FREEZE-FRAME and learn to consciously choose and perceive differently. Children actually love to do this because they feel that they have their own power. They get to go into their heart, think about what to do, and think about which choices they have. At this point in their development, children like to be absorbed in thought. So Freeze-Framing becomes a fun game.

This is how seven year old Blake describes life since practicing FREEZE-FRAME: *"I love it. There is nothing at all I don't feel good about in my life. I really feel good about it because I get to learn about the HeartMath. I learn to FREEZE-FRAME and stay in my heart better — like on Mondays I feel ugh, it's a school day. I don't like to get up so early and it's cold on school days, but I wouldn't want life without school — so I FREEZE-FRAME and it's easier to get up when I'm in my heart. Kids out of their hearts try to be real tough and bullish — they just don't like the way life goes. How do I know when they are out of their hearts? By the way their emotions go and they aren't in a really good mood."*

If a child keeps asking, "Is it time for the party yet?" when you've already told him the party is in two hours, or if he has to be reminded it's a school day not a weekend day, it's possible he is not yet developmentally qualified to engage in sequential thinking. Until then, projecting and highlighting consequences is necessary. For example, "On school days, you have to get up at 7:30 in order to wash up, get dressed, eat breakfast, and be out the door to catch the school bus by 8:30. If you keep dawdling you'll miss your bus."

Children can describe events which just happened, but find it hard to explain their choices while emotional. By ages six to eight children are able to see the progression of their emotions. They can start to comprehend the real issue — it's not the feeling itself that's the problem but how they choose to act out the feeling. Acknowledging feelings is important for healthy emotional development. Parents can assist by asking questions that encourage self-assessment. Self-assessment is pondering an outcome in the abstract, then electing a heart choice to accomplish the outcome.

Nine year old Debbie would get frustrated when her eighteen year old brother Steve teased her. During one episode, Debbie became so angry she threw her hair brush at Steve, missed, and broke a small window. Debbie knew her dad would be furious and contemplated what to do. She decided she would meet him at the bus stop, tell him what happened as they walked home together, and offer to pay for the window out of her allowance. Her father listened calmly and agreed to the plan. Debbie was pleased with her choice. Self-discipline is yielding to self-assessment and self-choice. The child is headed towards perceptions which require an even more complex application of ideas to real life interactions. This growth process gives her the ability to assess a situation with respect to its practical and ethical appropriateness, then make decisions concerning the world on the basis of that assessment. Launching the middle years of childhood with a solid common sense is what empowers a child to skillfully maneuver on the roads of life.

Seven Years Old

As caretakers, parents need to exhibit love and observe, guiding the seven year old's choices through his new sense of growing independence instead of solving all problems for him. With the additional brain cells, the seven year old is busy improving, strengthening, discovering himself. He has rather high standards and ideals. A seven year old loves to slow down and ponder things uninterrupted. In his moodiness he tends to worry about everything. If his questions about his anxieties go unanswered, the stress will stack. Seven year olds incline towards being gloomy and unhappy. Acknowledge this as a challenging year for your child and that he is not necessarily bluffing when he's sulking and pouting. Love him and communicate with him. Understandingly allow him to ask questions about all his worries. Then calmly and clearly answer these worries in a comprehensive manner. Worries can range from: I won't do well in school, my friend doesn't like me, my shirt is not red, an earthquake might happen, to what if my parents don't have enough money for food.

To help children release anxiety or worry, take them through the first few steps of HEART LOCK-IN or Freeze-Framing to help them feel their heart. Then say, *"Let's do something different this time. Let's gently stir and blend the feelings in our heart."* Keep the speed slow and rhythmic. You can say, *"The heart talks to everyone in their own special way. You might see or feel different colors or shapes or have new thoughts and ideas. As sad feelings come up, put them back into the heart, and stir them, like you are mixing paint. Let's do this for a few moments . . . (Pause) Then as you feel better, relax and soak in your heart. Feel like you are soaking in peace, in a nice heartwarming bath."*

Afterwards, you can ask your child if he would like to talk about how he feels or any new thoughts he has. If your child isn't verbal, he might like to write, draw or paint to express his feelings and thoughts. Always acknowledge and appreciate a child's efforts and expression of sincere feelings. That helps him respect his own feelings so he can understand them better, release them, and move on with life. Care within reason, and at the same time try not to overcare.

Eight Years Old

The eight year old has the opposite of seven year old characteristics. He is ready to utilize his new-found ideas, perceiving life's challenges with zest. His communication and relationships with all people are improving. His brightness and keenness are qualities of new emotional maturity. An eight year old can swiftly shift from one activity to another in wonderment of all experiences. Everything can seem brand new to him now that he can actively express his new perceptions of himself. He appreciates adults' company and is inquisitive about how they convey themselves, especially his parents.

When an eight year old gets frustrated, with all his extra gusto, he can become truly angry. After he calms down, help him shift back to his heart and have a heart talk on how to express his feelings differently. He is continuously searching for better directions in expressing himself. Heart praise and appreciation are welcome to an eight year old, for his efforts are often sincere. Appreciate an eight year old's flexibility and willingness to change for his parent's approval. His outgoing and fun-loving behavior also require room to run and play. Provide safe outside areas in which he can play. This can be a rewarding and fun year for both parent and child.

Nine Years Old

A nine year old takes himself seriously, wholeheartedly. He appears to want more challenges, so he actually needs more responsibilities. Parents need to access their intuition and find responsibilities equivalent to the child's maturity. He is so sincerely focused on perfecting his skills, that he will be glad to do the same task again and again, no matter what. Completion is a major concern, for a nine year old has tremendous determination. Help him stay balanced in the heart; if he is perceiving from the head he is likely to judge himself and others. He has new awareness with which to evaluate himself and others, so he can be very critical about individual actions. If he is in his head processors, he looks for worries and complaints. Give him fun games at home, and help him practice FREEZE-FRAME to develop his heart power. He will diligently make his efforts.

The concept of friendship is a top priority for a nine year old. She is a steadfast and faithful friend to play with. Emotionally, she sincerely cares and can feel she is responsible for hurting someone's feelings. She loves to have long heart-to-heart talks with her friends and parents, covering every subject matter imaginable. Communicate with your nine year old and help her feel understood. HeartMath tools will aid you and your child in closing any communication gap.

Ten Years Old

A ten year old loves and sincerely appreciates his parents. He delights in life and warmly participates in family activities. If he's basically self-secure, there is usually acceptance of all. He doesn't argue just to express and develop himself anymore. He seemingly loves school, friends, family outings, grandparents, and pets. Running, dancing, or any physical activity feels absolutely exulting to him. Indoors, a ten year old likes TV, music, video games, challenging board games, puzzles, dolls, models, painting, reading, and helping mom and dad.

While in his heart, his relationships and interactions are smooth and sociably fitting. When seeing life solely from a head perception, he can become surprisingly irritated with people. He may scream and yell, or kick the chair and slam the door as he exits a situation. He usually doesn't express verbal judgments because he's so sensitive to others judging and making fun of him. When he's in his heart, his honesty and sincere desire to do well should be appreciated by his parents. Often, his heart intelligence tells him if he is right or wrong, but his conscience likes to check with his parents to make sure he made the correct choice. Parents need to help the ten year old appreciate his own self-worth.

Eleven Years Old

Eleven year olds frequently react like pre-teens, which of course they are. They have contradictions with parents over many major and minor situations. Once more, this rebellion against parents, teachers, and authority figures is an expansion process. She is trying to define herself within a world that is changing as fast as she is. Choosing between parents' standards and peer criteria can be a difficult choice at times.

The eleven year old's ego spirit is just beginning to emerge, so expect some clumsiness, controversies, and stubbornness. This age can become confused about right and wrong choices. Eleven year olds who have practiced the HeartMath tools and have a heart understanding make a higher ratio of intelligent decisions. They are etching the ego self or spirit self. When heart intelligence is present, a child this age will often slow down enough to hear her still small voice, or if a parent is around, will ask questions. Emotions and hormones are just beginning to blossom.

Loving an eleven year old from a distance helps take the edges off verbal communication. Fewer edges mean less defiance, lying, disputes, fussing, or fighting about any issue. While communicating with pre-teens, send love, as they will be less likely to lie or fuss in a loving atmosphere. Children want help when they feel understood and respected. If a child feels safe, she will more likely tell the truth. Sincerely listen to her stressors and help her find some comprehension. Be understanding, as this is a difficult age.

Twelve Years Old

The classic twelve year old recoils to seek security within himself. Parents perceive this age as more bearable and friendlier. Twelve year olds are in the process of establishing their own self-identity: emotionally, mentally, and physically. The pre-frontal lobes are the last portion of the brain to develop, starting around age twelve. This part of the brain considers what is best for the collective whole, as well as for itself. It also entertains mathematical concepts that relate the part to the whole. If other developmental stages have not been completed, the growth of the pre-frontal lobes may be forestalled. Children who have mastered previous developmental stages can now grasp mathematical laws of probability (the likely occurrence of uncertain events) and geometry (the configuration and relationships between angles and forms), and then apply their meaning to life's events and situations. They can intuitively understand what non-linear chaos theory states — that there is an underlying order and meaning in chaos. Therefore they can feel more secure.

Major physical changes are going on inside a twelve year old child. Emotionally he is calmer as he steps back and observes, preparing himself for the teenage years. Girls are becoming interested in boys, but boys think the girl's interest is silly. Both are starting to request information and facts on the opposite sex. Friends are important, for they supply a sense of support and adventure. Twelve year olds generally have a passion for life, feeling new hope when perceiving from a heart perspective.

Is your pre-adolescent capable of creating a less stressful life as a teenager so her childlike spirit can stay alive and thrive? If she has developed creative resilience, challenging events will be perceived as just "waves of life." Heart intelligent skills are essential for teens to survive and prosper during this shift. Seeing from a heart perspective sincerely makes a difference. Teens who have not developed heart intelligence are insecure, lack hope and tend to view life pessimistically.

Increasing heart intelligence creates self-reliance that forms solid self-esteem. This serves as a buffer against stressors and social pressure. If a parent has raised a child wisely, there is a much greater likelihood of her returning home after exploring peers, school, and society with *less stress*. Seeing a pre-teen make mature choices definitely brings more tranquillity to a parent watching a child exit the house each day. To cultivate this maturity, continue to *love and observe from a distance* while your pre-teen explores life. When she's at home, exercise the benefits of sincerely listening and communicating.

If you are a parent or caretaker, practice the INTUITIVE LISTENING tool described in Chapter 7 with your child so you can give caring and effective answers. Listen to all people, including children, as you would like to be listened to. This establishes deeper respect. You don't have to agree with what they are saying, but waiting until they are done talking helps them feel heard. Often they come up with their own answers and solutions from their own heart intelligence just because you were sincerely listening to their heart. INTUITIVE LISTENING is real caring in action.

Before bedtime is often the best time for quiet family communication. Undistracted, you can discuss issues of importance, practice INTUITIVE LISTENING or other HeartMath tools, and share insights together.

Chapter 10

Understanding
The Teenage Shift

Until the sixties, the "teenage years" were not seen as such a stressful era. Nowadays teens deal with new feelings and emotions of adolescence in a fast-paced life. They have difficulty keeping up. The self is in a state of change. Self, defined as "I" or "Me," includes the self-images, feelings, concepts, thoughts, experiences, and relationships from which we derive our identity. If the abstract process of looking at one's self and one's own thoughts from a heart perception has not been developed, self-awareness will be suppressed. The adolescent DNA blueprint, the biological plan, is to define oneself in relation to peers and society.

From ages thirteen to nineteen, teens find themselves unaccustomed to a rapidly changing body, unfamiliar feelings, and impulsive thoughts. Their bodies produce enormous amounts of hormones. Emotions crank up, moodiness prevails. With all these fluxing insecurities, teens have to re-assess their identity all over again. Teens who have not learned to constructively address feelings are at the mercy of emotions, bouncing between bouts of anger and depression. Emotional disarray makes one susceptible to addictive habits, eating disorders, and reactive behavior.

In a poll among high school students in the U.S., more than 75% reported feeling stress weekly and often daily. U.S. students feel pressured to be good at many pursuits: school, making friends, sports, and having a job. In the study, 17% of girls and 10% of boys reported that they felt so much strain, stress, or pressure in the past month, "It was almost more than I could take." Scientific research has shown that prolonged exposure to stress can actually accelerate the aging of brain cells and lead to impairment of learning and memory. Stacked, stressful episodes damage and stunt development. They lead to extreme pessimism about life and hostile behavior. Studies have also shown that hostile teenagers are ten times more likely to have heart disease and die of cardiac arrest as adults.[13]

Teen Statistics

If we consider a few more statistics, a picture emerges of just how much pressure these kids are under. Highway accidents are the leading killer of teenagers. All told, 33% of drivers ages sixteen to twenty who were killed in accidents in 1994, registered blood alcohol levels of .10 or higher. More than one-third of the nation's teens drink alcohol weekly, while nearly half a million are binge drinkers whose weekly consumption averages fifteen drinks. During a break from writing this chapter, I saw an ABC-TV factoid stating, "38% of teens drank five or more alcoholic drinks in one sitting in the past two weeks."

Suicide is the second leading cause of death for people ages fifteen to twenty-four. Experts note that for every suicide, there are between 300 and 350 serious attempts made, and that 60% of all high school students say they have contemplated suicide. Girls try to commit suicide at a rate four to five times that of boys, although boys succeed more often. Rather than killing themselves over one incident, most suicidal teenagers are reacting to a culmination of pent-up frustrations and depression. Studies say that peer pressure is the main cause of teenage depression. I call it "peer momentum," a force propelling children to act as their peers do. Diagnosable mental disorders such as anxiety, depression, and schizophrenia are experienced by 18-22% of adolescents.

The third leading cause of death among teens is homicide. By 1992, teen homicide victims in the U.S. had increased 67% since 1986. Teenagers killing teenagers increased 85%. Guns were used in one of four teen deaths. Arrests of children younger than ten for violent crimes jumped 50%. What's more alarming is these figures are still on the increase. Violence is now responsible for more teen deaths each year than disease!

Why should these statistics be surprising when yet another poll found that one in five teens has not had even a ten minute conversation with a parent in the past month? The collapse of the American family in the past few decades is historically unprecedented in the U.S., and possibly in the world. In a 1994 nationwide poll of teenagers, conducted by the *New York Times* and *CBS News*, high percentages of youngsters said they could not share their worries or concerns with parents or any adults. Four in ten said their parents sometimes or often do not make time to help them — and many said the people they both trust and fear most are other teenagers. One typical sixteen year old response was, "Even when my parents are here, it's like they're not, because they don't have any time." Over 50% of teens who still eat dinner with their families say that TV is on during the meal and there is no real dinner conversation.

Parents may perceive their teen has no interest in them. Yet, polls show that parents remain a major influence through adolescence. Deep heart INTUITIVE LISTENING is an important, effective tool for parents of teenagers. Teenagers care deeply about what parents think. A *Reader's Digest* poll of high school seniors concluded that students with strong families are more successful in school. Teens want to be valued and respected. If parents are not there or have no time for them, they look to peers for their values and respect.

A teenager will search to find a meaningful frame of reference. A prerequisite for self-discovery is the adolescent's sequential figuring of what position she perceives to be her own. This warns a parent to be prepared for questioning, doubting, and testing of novel ideas. Although they doubt and rebel, teenagers yearn for acceptance. They want continual confirmation. Certain teens withstand peer momentum effortlessly, but most don't. Realize that teens are undergoing tremendous physiological and psychological changes in a society that is also changing extremely fast. They don't know what to think or feel.

With many hormonal changes affecting their feelings, teens have to rediscover what is their true heart versus what is just emotions. Their ability to discern this will be based on values they've internalized as a child. Most teenagers understand the consequences of certain actions. With the new hormonal confusion, they may lack common sense or act out behavior parents thought they had outgrown. A teenager who understood kindness as a nine year old may become rude and insolent as a thirteen year old. If after suffering the consequences of being rude, he goes to his heart for intuitive understanding, he'll remember the kindness he knew as a child or the care that someone has shown him and eventually adjust his behavior. However, teenagers in stress or whose hearts have shut down are often unable to find any intuitive perception. If people don't like them, they struggle with fight/flight reactions, withdrawing into depression, or fighting back with aggression. In a society that teaches children to be stressed and offers little perceived hope for the future, many teens say nobody cares, so they don't care. Yet they are looking for care and love. As one thirteen year old mother said, "Children are supposed to be the hope for the future; we don't see much hope in our own future, so we're having babies to love."

When children gaze into their future, what do they see? Pressure and stress. You get a job or go to college, face an insecure job market, bills pile up, responsibilities intensify, relationships crumble. From this perspective, teens often see only burdensome stress.

Common Sense Solutions

When it comes to the teenage years, most parents shake their heads in total exasperation. As I said earlier, parents feel teens don't listen and teens feel parents don't listen. So, there's a standoff. When emotions are surging, nothing seems to work. Can the HeartMath tools really cut through this impasse? Moods fluctuate, feelings of insecurity cascade, tears flow, sensitivities magnify, and flare-ups increase. The ratio of teen insecurities versus securities is determined by personality characteristics, experiences in life, family relationships, and subjection to peer momentum. A teen with heart perception, common sense, and communication ability journeys through these challenging years with less storm and stress. Practicing HeartMath tools helps balance the hormonal system, generating fulfillment and the heart-warming textures of real care. The results are regenerative for both parent and teen. Distinguishing the difference between real care, overcare, and no care will make a tremendous difference as you traverse these difficult years.

Teens need parents who remain sturdy, sincere, and conscientious. They require love and care to leap over the walls of confusion that society has constructed. Recognizing this, the prime task of a parent is to provide teenagers with a sense of individual assurance to counteract all the uncertainty. This builds maturity and understanding.

A meaningful relationship with a balanced, caring adult supplies a teen with an understanding of direction and purpose. It fulfills her desire for acceptance and love. Balanced care is a source of strength in times of stress. Frequently it can lessen the feeling of being alone during this chaotic period. By building a friendly, accepting relationship with teenagers, you heighten the chance that they will give your heart values earnest respect. A teen who has acquired confidence from prior successes is less liable to be swept up in peer momentum. Teenagers who know they are loved and worthy will not need to look for security from their environment.

HeartMath tools aid both parents and teens with a knowledge of how to gather their feelings to form efficient choices. Demonstrate how to release overcares and find balanced care for yourself and for them. Teaching teenagers HeartMath helps them see a different possible outcome and understand deeper consequences of feelings and actions for themselves. It enables teens to harness their energies and envision their future with robust emotions and happy feelings. They will see they do have a choice.

In discussing HeartMath with children twelve to nineteen, it helps to talk about how hormones affect our moods and behavior. Explain that HeartMath power tools help teenagers (and adults) stay in balance as they go through emotional mood swings. The tools enable you to use heart intelligence for traveling through the teenage years with less stress and more fun. Talk about care and overcare and areas where you have overcared. Your teen will probably be able to help you easily identify your overcares and may even tell you, "I've told you that you worry too much." Help your teen identify her overcares, the areas where she worries, feels anxious, or gets distraught and feels drained. Ask your teenager if anyone has meant a lot to her in life, someone who truly cared without overcaring. Discuss that person's qualities. Especially share with teens how FREEZE-FRAME has helped you. Practice the steps of FREEZE-FRAME with your teen. Help her understand how to recognize where her caring was taken to inefficient extremes.

Encourage her to practice FREEZE-FRAME until she feels a release, and has a clearer perception with a feeling of security coming back. Support her in listening to her own heart intelligence to understand what true care would be in her situation. As teenagers release overcare, they gain tremendous power to put care in action and listen to their common sense. They find new care and passion to be all they can be. Talk about the potency of true care, how you feel when you are truly caring about others versus how you feel when you overcare, or when your heart cuts off and you don't care anymore. Help teens shape their core values with the power of true care from the heart.

Thirteen Years Old

Thirteen year olds will internalize their feelings and retract from the world instantly. Oftentimes they retreat to their rooms, uncertain about themselves, other people, and life in general. They thought they already had it together, but now are unsure and are not secure enough to display their frail self. A thirteen year old constantly worries about self, body, and image. When stuck in his head, a thirteen year old becomes despondent, feeling things are only getting worse. Teens frequently brood about parents not caring, listening, or understanding. Remember, he is only trying to discover himself, so a thirteen year old may be rather reclusive at home. When a teen is in his heart, he seemingly enjoys discovering himself. All life's challenges are seen as creative resistances instead of stacked stress.

Teach your teen the HEART LOCK-IN technique described in Chapter 1. Help him see what a powerful tool love is, for getting out of a bad mood and for feeling appreciation for himself. Explain why people have to love and feel good about themselves first to really love others. When a teenager is having a relationship or communication problem with a friend, teacher, or parent, suggest he do a five minute HEART LOCK-IN. Offer to do it with your teen. See if sending love doesn't help everyone's mood, bring new intuitive understanding, and help the relationship. Discuss the HEART LOCK-IN results with your teenager.

Friends are a delight for a thirteen year old entering the social arena. There is increasing attraction to the opposite sex, while talking, dating, and parties are a social enjoyment. School is an acceptable place to be for a thirteen year old, considering it is a situation away from parents. It doesn't have much to do with teachers.

Thirteen year olds may argue again and again with parents to get what they want or think they want. From their perspective, they feel they have good reasons for wanting whatever the dispute is over. Often they will endure a parent's demands, feeling they have to, but inside feel quite misunderstood. Communicate and love them; guide their conscience, which is now a recognizable part of themselves. In a loving and secure environment, thirteen year olds want to tell the truth and often will do so, although they may tell a white lie to save their face or someone else's. All in all, remember that this year presents a genuine and serious growth challenge in finding themselves. Love your thirteen year old and encourage him through this expansive year.

Fourteen Years Old

Fourteen year olds are more expressive and outgoing, so communicating with them is much easier. They love activities, friends, after school sports, and clubs. Fourteen is an excellent age to teach FREEZE-FRAME or reinstate the practice of this tool. Teach your fourteen year old Freeze-Framing by using a combination of the instructions for ages seven to twelve in Chapter 9 and the adult instructions in Chapter 3. Read a few paragraphs on FREEZE-FRAME with your teen. Discuss the scientific basis of the tool and areas where it could be of benefit to him and the whole family. Especially share how the tool has helped you. Be honest. Teenagers like straight heart talk. Discuss and make a plan together of how and where you both can experiment with the tool to see if it helps. Use it for creative projects, not just for stressful situations. Agree to remind each other to FREEZE-FRAME. Make it an adventure and compare notes on the results of being the director of your own movie.

As you discuss each other's insights, you build respect and understanding, and deepen a bond of friendship. I wrote my first book, *The How To Book of Teen Self Discovery,* in simple language and straight heart talk that teens understand. In that book I discuss typical teen situations, like dealing with peer pressure, schoolwork, sorting out relationship problems, communicating, and finding out who you really are. The book is written for teenagers to better understand themselves, but it helps them understand their parents as well and facilitates teen/adult bonding.

A heart-intelligent fourteen year old will make more effective choices. She defines herself apart from her family so there will still be differences of opinion. Through deep heart listening, parents can communicate. Fourteen year olds can't wait to verbalize and express themselves. Their lives are very busy with activities and frequently they prefer to be with friends. Nevertheless, teens like and require a secure place to retreat. Heart understanding parents need to help their action-packed fourteen year olds find balance in their lives.

Fifteen to Nineteen Years Old

Reading the alarming facts and figures on teens, we know something is extremely challenging for them. Those who lack trusting relationships with meaningful adults in their lives naturally seek out peers. But their peers are caught in the same situation, so teens don't acquire any advanced insights. Those who have secure perceptions, feeling they can rely on the significant adults in their lives, are notably more resistant to unhealthy peer momentum. From fifteen to nineteen years old, life will have new ups and downs and learning curves.

As I mentioned earlier, the current fashion of teens is to wear oversized pants so baggy they often fall down. One father I know was disgusted watching his fifteen year old son constantly pull his pants up or walk bow-legged to keep his pants from falling to his knees. He was worried that his son's hips would become deformed. The boy refused to change pants because the cool dudes wore that style. The father was afraid that if he yielded on the baggy pants, next might come the pierced ear, tattoo, or mohawk hairdo. The father finally realized, with sincere care and understanding, that he could meet the boy halfway. He bought him a belt so he would still be in style, but not injure himself. Parents need to try to meet teens halfway; their lives are constantly changing so help them make it fun.

Sixteen year olds are more relaxed and secure with themselves. Before this year, teenagers are more on the take side of life instead of the give side. Sixteen is the turning point when they gravitate toward caring about others and family. They tend to want harmony in relationships and appreciate what is given to them. A "sweet sixteen" year old can be a friendly, positive person with whom you want to communicate. Sixteen year olds cross a platform, having finally reached a stage of growth where they feel competent. They can even understand adults' stress and have compassion for them. By no means are they adults yet; they still need parental guidance.

Each stage of growth is intended by the DNA blueprint to prepare the teenager to be a contributing member of society who understands the natural laws and principles of life. As teens approach seventeen, eighteen, and nineteen, they emerge with sounder identities, more emotional stability, and fewer hormonal swings. They have more clarity expressing feelings in words, so their sense of life is on the rise. As self-security and self-reliance increase, they become more fulfilled. Parents can communicate with them and frequently be their teen's friend. They can also be a parent's friend. Having HeartMath tools, you can help fix problems together and derive workable solutions. Using heart intelligence, the spirit feels free, capable, and limitless. The self relies on its own system. A family spawns and nurtures the securities teens build in the heart. That inside security is the feeling of home. Heart-empowered parents and children live an existence of balance and fulfillment. From the end of adolescence through adulthood, the blueprint dictates that the time has come to use their own common sense to meet the challenges of life. The question is: Are they prepared?

Conclusion

If parents practice HeartMath tools day-to-day and make them a part of their lives, just like bathing, brushing teeth, or cooking healthy meals, children will think of using the tools as a natural way of living — a healthy and normal lifestyle. Stress and anxiety are not healthy or "normal," although many believe otherwise because stress has become the social norm. Even adults who think living with an overload of stress is normal do not want their child to lead a stressful life. Parents sincerely want their child, whether five or fifty years old, to be happy.

Children living from heart intelligence gain insights and solutions to problems. They profit from a new level of self-empowerment. There really is hope. People do have choice. Whether it's a problem with a parent, friend, or with thoughts that arise and take hold, people do have a choice in how they perceive that experience. One's perspective in the moment influences which direction a child or adult take. Perceptions and feelings are an individual's truth in the moment.

It's important to understand that a child is continuously changing. No child forever moves in the way a parent prefers. Remember, intuition is the ability to "see into it" and receive the most expansive possible perspective. *Build your heart muscle by practicing the tools on small stresses.* This will prepare you for the more difficult issues.

It's so important in the global paradigm shift, with stress increasing everywhere, that parents take personal responsibility for their own self-care. That means parenting your own self. Apply the common-sense advice you would give your children to help them be happier and release frustration, worry, anxiety, anger, stress — to yourself.

A Parenting Manual is for parenting anyone, including yourself. The tools are scientifically developed and proven to keep one's child-like spirit alive and happy, so that life can be the quality adventure it is meant to be. In practicing HeartMath tools and principles, the most important factor is *consistency*. If parents are consistent as role models, using the tools to maintain emotional balance and gain new perspectives, then children will follow that consistency and self-empower as time goes on. It doesn't mean they won't swing back and forth in attitude or never be a challenge — that's part of the growth process. If children never had challenges, they wouldn't adjust to life. My intention is to show how challenges can be met from the heart — with strength and courage instead of fear and despair.

As I mentioned earlier, children sincerely need to feel parents are open to understanding them. The strong "peer momentum" today propels many children to reject parental values, join gangs, or become self-destructive. Remember, there is a lack of adult role models to show children how to deal with life's challenges in balanced, constructive ways. As I've said repeatedly, the biggest problem according to kids is: "Adults don't listen." HeartMath tools show you how to listen and understand your child. If you really love your child, you will listen and care — and maintain consistent bottom-line rules.

Parenting can be a very hard job. Without the heart, many parents give up, burn-out, let their kids go, or just stop caring. You are preparing a child for life, and life has laws. There are laws of physics that govern the movement and relationships between matter and energy on Earth. There are also laws of behavior that govern relationships between people.

A surprisingly large number of difficult and problematic children do become happy, successful adults. One young man I know was headed for a life of trouble. It started when he was nine and several older boys wanted to break into a neighboring house to steal whiskey while the owners were on vacation. They needed a smaller person to hoist up and crawl through the window. The nine year old obliged. One of the older boys bragged to his sister about their prank and she told her parents. That night his parents learned of his misdeed. The boy had to confess to the neighbors about his stealing when they returned from vacation. He never broke into anyone's house again and for years thereafter felt embarrassed whenever he saw those neighbors. However, at fifteen, this same boy was getting D's and F's in high school, was abusing liquor, and was getting into further trouble, so his parents threatened to send him to a boot-camp type military school. With this reality before him, he could see his life was going nowhere and realized that he wanted to change. He focused on developing his talents in music and went to college. Years later, that troubled teenager is now the president of a publishing company and a leading speaker on reducing stress in business and in the military.

Research indicates that happy adults who were difficult as children, or grew up in stressed environments, have one thing in common — supportive relationships with positive adult role models. As a result they developed creative *resiliency*. A major difference between children who are resilient and those who are not is their perception of what happens to them.

An aware parent loves all children he or she meets and interacts with — for you are a caretaker for those moments in time. Now is the time for people to unite within their families and their communities. Many schools and cities are making an effort in this direction, but too often it takes a crisis to bring them together. Until then, neighbors frequently don't know who lives next door. In a crisis, neighbors try to feel as if it is "all one big backyard," but need help finding effective ways to create and sustain this sense.

References

1. *Webster's® New World Dictionary.* 3rd college ed., ed. V. Neufeldt. 1993, New York: Prentice Hall.

2. McCraty, R., M. Atkinson, and W. A. Tiller, *New electrophysiological correlates associated with intentional heart focus.* Subtle Energies, 1995. **4**(3):251-262.

3. McClelland, D.C., *Some reflections on two psychologies of love.* Journal of Personality, 1986. **54**(2):334-353.

4. Ironson, G., *et al.*, *Effects of anger on left ventricular ejection fraction in coronary artery disease.* American Journal of Cardiology, 1992. **70**(3):281-285.

5. Rein, G. and R. M. McCraty, *Long term effects of compassion on salivary IgA.* Psychosomatic Medicine, 1994. **56**(2):171-172.

6. Zachariae, R., *Monocyte chemotactic activity in sera after hypnotically induced emotional states.* Scandinavian Journal of Immunology, 1991. **34**(1):71-79.

7. Pearce, J. C., *Evolution's End: Claiming the Potential of Our Intelligence.* 1992, San Francisco:Harper Collins.

8. McCraty, R., *et al.*, *The effects of emotions on short term heart rate variability using power spectrum analysis.*

9. McCraty, R., *et al.*, *Head-Heart Entrainment: A Preliminary Survey.*

10. Shimony, A., *The Reality of the Quantum World.* Scientific American, 1988. **258**(1):46-48.

11. Burrows, G. *Stress and the Professional.* In *Seventh International Montreux Congress on Stress*, 1994. Montreux, Switzerland: American Institute of Stress.

12. Eadie, B.J., *Embraced by the Light.* 1992, Placerville, CA: Gold Leaf Press.

13. Siegler, I., *et al.*, *Hostility During Late Adolescence Predicts Coronary Risk Factors at Mid-life.* Am J Epidemiol, 1992. **136**(2):146-154.

About the Editors...

Sara Hatch Paddison, editor

Sara Paddison brings her experience as an author, a mother, her background in psychology and elementary education from East Carolina University, and her extensive work with Doc Lew Childre, to her editorial role for *A Parenting Manual*. Sara serves as vice president and chief financial officer of the nonprofit Institute of HeartMath (IHM). She is author of *The Hidden Power of the Heart*, now in its third printing, upon which IHM's successful Heart Empowerment® seminars are based. *The Hidden Power of the Heart* tells Sara's personal story of self-transformation using HeartMath tools.

Deborah Rozman, Ph.D., contributing editor

Psychologist, author, and IHM Executive Director, Deborah is perhaps best known for her classic books for children, educators and parents, including *Meditating With Children*. As a leader in educational psychology, she founded a successful, innovative school specializing in creativity and intuitive development in children. Deborah develops and presents IHM programs throughout the U.S. and Canada, and is a frequent keynote speaker.

Bruce Cryer, contributing editor

Bruce Cryer is the editor and spokesperson for Doc Lew Childre's *FREEZE-FRAME: Fast Action Stress Relief, A Scientifically Proven Technique*. As Executive Director of IHM's corporate division, Bruce develops and teaches practical programs for implementing FREEZE-FRAME® and Inner Quality Management® — activating care, effectiveness and increased productivity in businesses. Bruce is also a father and writes children's stories.

With the pace of change in society accelerating, people need proven, practical tools to empower themselves — to manage anger and still speak their truth, to revitalize relationships, and to increase their power to make efficient decisions. Simply stated, people want to feel good! At the Institute of HeartMath (IHM), we have looked into our hearts, and found the answers to be there — in the heart. Our mission is to put the heart back into people's daily lives.

IHM is a nonprofit, innovative research and education organization, incorporated in 1991 in Boulder Creek, California by Doc Lew Childre. We have pioneered new biomedical research that has profound implications in helping you become more effective and fulfilled in all that you do. Our workshops and customized training programs have helped thousands of people and hundreds of organizations across the United States and around the world break through to greater levels of clarity, creativity and intuitive insight, reduce stress, improve communication, and enhance overall well-being.

Our Boulder Creek programs provide ample private time for relaxation, recreation, and reflection. Skilled, experienced facilitators lead you on a full, in-depth learning adventure that blends classroom instruction with personal and interactive exercises. You'll explore the fun of new friendships in a setting where you can truly be yourself and enjoy the beauty of nature. Whether you attend a program at IHM or one that is sponsored by your organization closer to home, you'll find new insights on how to follow your heart towards greater personal empower-ment.

For complete information on IHM training programs, contact:
INSTITUTE OF HEARTMATH
14700 West Park Avenue, Boulder Creek, California 95006
(408) 338-8700 fax (408) 338-9861
Internet: hrtmath@netcom.com
Visit our Website: http://www.webcom.com/hrtmath

155

TEACHING CHILDREN TO LOVE
55 GAMES AND FUN ACTIVITIES FOR
RAISING BALANCED CHILDREN IN UNBALANCED TIMES
By Doc Lew Childre

    Teaching Children To Love offers parents, teachers, and child care providers a complete hands-on guide for having fun while developing positive, healthy, life skills in children of all ages. Presented in a step-by-step format for family, classroom, and youth program settings. Based on the tools and techniques presented in *A Parenting Manual.*
    Item #1145 $14.95

THE HOW TO BOOK OF TEEN SELF DISCOVERY
HELPING TEENS FIND BALANCE, SECURITY & ESTEEM
By Doc Lew Childre

    Find help, hope, and solutions in this book written specifically for teens. Approved as a textbook in the state of California, *Teen Self Discovery* offers easy tools for developing inner-security and communication and listening skills, while managing emotions and reactions. Teens learn how to make positive choices and successfully meet the challenges of today's world.
    Item #1065 $8.95

SELF EMPOWERMENT
THE HEART APPROACH TO STRESS MANAGEMENT
By Doc Lew Childre

    A comprehensive view of today's social issues and how each individual can make a positive difference. An essential book for understanding that making changes within yourself is the first step toward world change.

"The message is a strong one and the methodology can be understood by many. The potential release of positive energy is formidable."
    J. Tracy O'Rourke, Chairman and CEO
    Varian Associates, Inc.
    Item #1120 $13.95

This looks great!

THE HIDDEN POWER OF THE HEART
ACHIEVING BALANCE AND FULFILLMENT IN A STRESSFUL WORLD
By Sara Paddison

A warm and fascinating account of a journey through the heart to find more love and happiness. Told with a simple yet profound understanding of spirituality, our holographic universe and the role of the heart in claiming our "intuitive intelligence."

"Sara Paddison's book will revitalize the truth whereby one can not only consult one's heart but can actually listen to what it says. This book should be required reading."

Dr. Vernon H. Mark, Director Emeritus
Boston City Hospital
Item #1060 $11.95

HEART ZONES

By Doc Lew Childre

Based on advanced research on the physical and emotional effects of music on the listener, *Heart Zones* is an intelligent blending of creativity and science. This four song musical composition designed to boost vitality and facilitate mental and emotional balance is the first music of its kind—'Designer Music'—to reach the *Billboard* charts where it remained for a year.

Cassette	Item #3170	$9.95
CD	Item #3175	$15.95

"Like a psychological cup of coffee without the side effects."
USA Today

SPEED OF BALANCE
A MUSICAL ADVENTURE FOR EMOTIONAL & MENTAL REGENERATION
By Doc Lew Childre

Doc Lew Childre's follow-up to his landmark release *Heart Zones*. *Speed of Balance* * features eight new songs that have been arranged to create a cascading effect that leaves the listener with more energy and feeling ready to move on with life. Jazz enthusiasts, classical lovers, and even rock-n-rollers find it revitalizing and entertaining. *Speed of Balance* represents the next step in music scientifically designed to make you feel good as well as entertain.

Cassette	Item #3250	$9.95
CD	Item #3255	$15.95

*A recent study showed that people can raise their own levels of the anti-aging hormone DHEA by practicing the new CUT-THRU technique and listening to *Speed of Balance*.

FREEZE-FRAME® PRODUCTS & PROGRAMS

The FREEZE-FRAME technique is a core tool in the HeartMath system. It provides a foundation which all the training programs and retreats are built.

FREEZE-FRAME WORKSHOPS

FREEZE-FRAME workshops provide hands-on instruction and practical applications of the FREEZE-FRAME technique. These powerful and practical half-day programs are available on-site for corporations, governmental agencies, and public institutions through certified HeartMath® trainers and at IHM's research facility. Call for more information.

FREEZE-FRAME RESEARCH/TRAINING VIDEO

This powerful training video features an in-depth presentation of the leading-edge scientific research behind FREEZE-FRAME, along with step-by-step instruction and personal interviews from professionals illustrating the impact and diverse applications of this innovative, self-management technique. Used alone or as part of meetings, special programs or training sessions, this high-quality tool is an excellent resource for trainers, consultants, and organizations in need of stress management, team building, improved customer service, organizational development, enhanced communication skills, and project planning. *Item #4010 $595.00 plus shipping and handling (Item #4012 $40.00 preview fee), lease/purchase agreements available*

FREEZE-FRAME WORKSHEETS

A convenient, easy-to-use form for written FREEZE-FRAME exercises. Encourages faster development of FREEZE-FRAME skill.
Item #1045 $6.95 (pad of 50 worksheets)

FREEZE-FRAME: FAST ACTION STRESS RELIEF
A SCIENTIFICALLY PROVEN TECHNIQUE

By Doc Lew Childre

This best seller from the HeartMath series offers a proven technique for managing stress, improving communication skills, and increasing your personal effectiveness. It's hard to believe something so easy can make such a difference in your life — but it can!

"If you're upset, the heart feels it. What you can do in the moment to calm yourself down is called Freeze-Frame."
Dr. Donna Willis, NBC News' *"Today Show"*
Item #1040 $9.95

FREEZE-FRAME AUDIOBOOK

The FREEZE-FRAME Audiobook, which includes musical compositions from Doc Lew Childre's latest "Designer Music" release, is invaluable to anyone who prefers listening to reading. Includes step-by step instruction of the FREEZE-FRAME technique by Bruce Cryer, one of the nation's leading business consultants.

". . . a research based system for taking charge of our own well-being and peace of mind."
The Voice (Richmond, VA)
Item #3145 $16.95

FREEZE-FRAME INNER FITNESS SYSTEM

The FREEZE-FRAME Inner Fitness System provides you with everything you need to start your own "Inner Fitness" program. Develop the mental and emotional "muscles" you need to renew your zest for life, boost your energy level and achieve maximum potential. This special offer includes:

- *FREEZE-FRAME* video and book
- *Heart Zones* (designer music)
- FREEZE-FRAME Worksheets
  an $83.00 value

| With cassette | Item #1043 | $59.95 |
| With CD | Item #1044 | $64.95 |

CUT-THRU® PRODUCTS & PROGRAMS

HeartMath's latest technique, CUT-THRU, is simple, powerful, and life changing. CUT-THRU shows you how to quickly recoup from energy drains and renew your power.

CUT-THRU WORKSHOPS

CUT-THRU workshops provide hands-on instruction and practical applications of the CUT-THRU technique. These powerful and practical half-day programs are available on-site for corporations, governmental agencies, and public institutions through certified HeartMath trainers and at IHM's research facility. Call 1-800-450-9111 for more information.

CUT-THRU BOOK
ACHIEVE TOTAL SECURITY AND MAXIMUM ENERGY
A SCIENTIFICALLY PROVEN INSIGHT ON
HOW TO CARE WITHOUT BECOMING A VICTIM

Millions experience worry, anxiety, or insecurity regarding people and issues they care about. CUT-THRU provides a powerful solution. Learn to prevent overcare for mental and emotional empowerment and freedom. Unleash free energy to increase your quality of life and health.

Item #1023 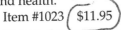 $11.95

CUT-THRU AUDIOBOOK

This simple technique which eliminates the "burnout" syndrome is now available as an audiobook. You'll be surprised at how easy it is to "CUT-THRU" long-standing emotional issues and even what seem to be "unsolvable" situations, just by practicing this proven technique. A valuable investment for anyone who wants to be in control of their mental, emotional, and physical well-being.

Item #3120 $16.95

CUT-THRU ASSET/DEFICIT WORKSHEETS

A convenient, easy-to-use form for practicing the CUT-THRU technique. Helps you define issues, conflicts, and events that are draining your energy and determine how to "CUT-THRU" to new levels of insights and solutions. Transform deficits into assets.

Item #1024 $6.95

PLANETARY

Ordering Information:

Phone • Fax • Mail

Please send check, money order or credit card information to:

PLANETARY PUBLICATIONS
P.O. Box 66 • Boulder Creek, California, 95006
800-372-3100/408-338-2161/Fax 408-338-9861

- For convenience, place your order using our toll-free number
  — 800-372-3100, 24 hours a day, 7 days a week.
- Visa, Mastercard, Discover Card, and American Express
  accepted. Please include expiration date, card number, full
  name on card, and signature.
- Shipping and handling cost:
  $5.25 for first item,
  $1.00 each additional item.
- California residents include 7.25% sales tax.
  (Santa Cruz County residents include 8.25% sales tax.)
- Foreign Orders:
  Call or fax for accurate shipping rates.

Visit our Website:
http://www.webcom.com/hrtmath

1-800-372-3100

Self Enpowerment # 1120 $13.95

...publishers of The HeartMath Series